CORPORATE
OVATIONS

Praise for **Corporate Ovations**

"*Corporate Ovations* thoroughly covers it from A to Z if you want to learn to give an effective presentation. You'll find lots of great ideas to make you a more powerful communicator. It will teach you to put the audience first and that will help make you a first-class speaker."

> —MARK SANBORN, Award-winning Speaker and Best-selling Author of *The Fred Factor* and *You Don't Need a Title to Be a Leader*

"Russ and Kevin share powerful principles for delivering outstanding presentations. When you read this book, you'll never approach presentations the same way. I highly recommend it!"

> —JON GORDON, Best-selling Author of *The Energy Bus* and *The Seed*

"Stop winging your presentations! Great, engaging presentations don't just happen. *Corporate Ovations* delivers proven methods to prepare your message, engage your audience, and leave a lasting impression. The tools in this book will help you think and prepare differently for your next business meeting or speaking engagement."

> —HEATHER TROTTER, National Account Sales Director, Coca-Cola

"One of the best books on communication that I have ever read. It is simple, practical and provides extremely useful advice. A must-read!"

> —MARCELA MARTIN, Executive Vice President & CFO, Fox International Channels

"Finally there's a book that not only shows you how to make an effective presentation but also helps you become a great presenter. With the valuable resources inside this book, your speeches will never be the same and neither will your audiences. Follow the keys in this 'must-have' book and you'll receive many *Corporate Ovations*."

> —CRAIG VALENTINE, 1999 World Champion of Public Speaking and Author of *World Class Speaking*

"Ten years and three corporations later, I am still bringing Russ and Kevin to my workforce . . . they never let us down . . . I can show ROI on this stuff!"

> —LACEY NEEF-HEDRICK, Talent Development Advisor, Champion Technologies

"*Corporate Ovations* is the perfect blueprint to delivering great presentations. It is a must-have tool for your personal or professional tool box."

> —KEVIN MCNABB, Vice President of Sports & Leisure, Academy Sports + Outdoors

"This book has it all! Russ and Kevin have created the new 'go-to' handbook on public speaking and presentations. *Corporate Ovations* has an easy to read, easy to implement style. . . . Excellent for those early on in their careers as well as seasoned professionals. I am highly recommending that we augment our presentation skills classes with a mandatory reading of this book."

> —JOSEPH NAPOLITANO, Director, Strategic Account Management, Tokyo Electron America

"This is a practical and well-researched book. I loved the links to see 'live' examples of concepts I just read about in each chapter. Kevin and Russ provide easy to remember formulas (CABA, MAS, etc.) to help the reader remember important elements of delivering a presentation. This is a great resource for both novice and more seasoned presenters who may need some new ideas."

—Darlene Masci, Global Trainer and Instructional Designer, Hewlett-Packard Corporation

"In a time when personal interaction is subsiding to digital communication, guidance for proper human connection during presentations is essential to succeed in the business world. Novice to expert presenters will benefit from the first-rate pathway defined in *Corporate Ovations*."

—Tom Stanek, Senior Director of Sales and Marketing, GTECH Corporation

"I have known Russ and Kevin for over 20 years. Their approach to training and effective presentations is thorough, fun and most importantly, accurate. If you're good at giving presentations, they will help make you great. If you've never presented, they will get you started in a way that makes a novice feel confident. *Corporate Ovations* is a must for anyone who wants to make a great impression in a professional way!"

—Tom Lucas, Director of International Human Resources, National Instruments

"Russ and Kevin use the *Corporate Ovations* techniques as they present this material to you, making it both incredibly useful and hard to put down. They not only give you the ideas and information, but they supply links to videos showing their methods in action. Whether you are new to public speaking and presentations or are a seasoned veteran, this book is for you."

—Dr. Dave Koppel, Senior Pastor, Palm Valley Lutheran Church

"I enjoyed reading *Corporate Ovations*. The authors translate their experience into valuable advice to improve our public speaking skills. They provide solid guidance on how to connect with the audience while communicating our message, and by breaking down each aspect of a presentation, they offer techniques and tools to engage the audience and achieve our goals. The book is filled with practical examples illustrating each area of focus."

—SCOTT BRANDT, Chief Information Officer, Office of the Texas Secretary of State

"*Corporate Ovations* offers solid, practical strategies for mastering every part of a professional presentation. Whether you're making your first boardroom presentation, or you're a seasoned executive, this book will polish your skills and inspire the confidence to powerfully communicate your message."

—MINDY AUDLIN, Award-winning Speaker and Author of What If It All Goes RIGHT?

"I found *Corporate Ovations* to be an interesting and informative read. It is a straightforward, common sense approach to delivering presentations that your audience will love. I particularly look forward to incorporating the 'Halo Effect' into my presentations, knowing my audience wants me to win."

—CARY K. RABB, President, Wag-a-Bag, Inc.

"*Corporate Ovations* is for everyone! It can help anyone overcome their fear and develop self-confidence with techniques for effective public speaking!"

—T.K. LEE, Managing Director, Asia Franchise Networks, Singapore

"The blueprint for success in sales' most critical area—impactful presenting—is in your hands. The ability to effectively and powerfully communicate differentiates, no matter your title or field, and *Corporate Ovations* clearly and methodically leads you through the steps to mastery. I have worked with the authors—outstanding in their field—for years and entrusted hundreds to their program. Engaging, practical and fun, you'll find no better guide to powerful presentations."

—TONI NOTTINGHAM, Director of Learning, Ellucian

"Russ and Kevin—and everyone on the iSpeak team—have been consummate, passionate professionals, which is why I have recommended them to clients seeking to improve their presentation skills. This book is a fine complement to their work. It's full of practical tips that take the mystery out of effective public speaking."

—DEBORAH HARNER, Manager, Global People
Development, Invesco Ltd.

"I love *Corporate Ovations*! I have been in the speaker industry for almost 10 years and I wish I had this book from the beginning! *Corporate Ovations* is the go-to guide to create powerful presentations that are sure to please your audiences, and lets you perform at your top potential. I read *Corporate Ovations* the night before a large National Sales Conference, and by applying their strategies, I nailed my keynote!"

—URSULA MENTJES, #1 Best-selling Author of *Selling
with Intention* and Founder of www.salescoachnow.com

"Effective presentations mean the difference between getting your way or not. And Russ Peterson and Kevin Karschnik show you how to make presentations effective."

—HERNAN LOPEZ, President & CEO, Fox International
Channels

"In the corporate world today, the ability to deliver dynamic and influential presentations is a crucial skill for any leader or aspiring leader. In *Corporate Ovations*, Kevin and Russ have compiled the ultimate guide to best practices on the subject. Their expertise and facilitation are an integral part of our company's overall leadership development strategy."

—MARGIE POOLE, Senior Organizational Development Consultant, CenterPoint Energy

"*Corporate Ovations* is full of the hard-to-find wisdom that makes presenters enjoy presenting and presentations so engaging and memorable. It doesn't only go over the most critical pitfalls, it tells you in very specific terms and through specific examples how to easily jump over the hurdles and win the right responses from your audience. This book is designed for easy digestion and acquisition of brilliant speaking practices. I'll be reading and re-reading this book before every presentation I give from now on!"

—REUT SCHWARTZ-HEBRON, Founder of Key Change Institute, Author of *The Art and Science of Changing People Who Don't Want to Change*

"Writers typically just share their thoughts with the reader in an effort to create emotions that might lead to change or improve performance. Russ and Kevin have gone a step further in this book. They share with the reader their combined wisdom; and motivate us to improve our public speaking. That's why this book is a rarity; it is both educational and inspirational. I highly recommended it to every level of public speaker from beginner to veteran."

—PAUL A. SLATTERY, Founder NxtGEN (Ireland) and Professional Speaker

"Karschnik and Peterson have created a great tool that is helpful for anyone who speaks in any kind of public setting. They have found a way to convey the energy, message and tips of their 'live' educational sessions into an easy to read, easy to implement guide for speakers of all levels of experience. The quotes are wonderful nuggets of wisdom that help the message sink in to the reader. Our team's ability to deliver our message has become significantly better after working through this roadmap."

—Ann Jerome, Chief Operating Officer, Ronald McDonald House Charities

"*Corporate Ovations* is a thorough guide for making effective presentations. Whether you are a novice with that fear-of-failure syndrome or a seasoned veteran, you will find the material fascinating and useful. Russ and Kevin have knocked it out of the park with this one."

—Michael Oldham, Vice President of Sales, Sysco Central Texas

CORPORATE
OVATIONS

Your Roadmap to More Effective Presentations

Kevin Karschnik   Russ Peterson Jr.

Discovery Tree Press

Corporate Ovations: Your Roadmap to More Effective Presentations

Copyright © 2013, Kevin Karschnik and Russ Peterson Jr.

Published by
Discovery Tree Press
3000 Joe DiMaggio Blvd, Suite 81
Round Rock, TX 78665

www.DiscoveryTreePress.com

ISBN–13: 978-1-940039-00-8

Cover and Interior Design: Desktop Miracles, Inc.

Publisher's Cataloging-In-Publication Data
(Prepared by The Donohue Group, Inc.)

Karschnik, Kevin.
    Corporate ovations : your roadmap to more effective presentations / Kevin Karschnik, Russ Peterson, Jr.
        p. : ill. ; cm.
    Includes bibliographical references and index.
    ISBN: 978-1-940039-00-8

    1. Business presentations.   2. Public speaking.
3. Speech anxiety.   I. Peterson, Russ.   II. Title.

HF5718.22   K37 2013
                                                        658.4/52

Printed in the United States of America

For Tracy, Kip, and Kait.
I am a blessed husband and father.
Love, Dad

For Cheree, Russell, and Cassidy,
Thank you for all your love and support.
Love, Dad

Table of Contents

Foreword

Working in the game of baseball is fun. I don't know how else to describe what I do. As the owner of two minor league baseball teams, the Round Rock Express and the Corpus Christi Hooks, it is an honor and a privilege to bring joy to people's lives.

Folks come out to the ballpark for a myriad of reasons. These reasons range from escaping the problems of life, watching players chase the dream of becoming a major leaguer, spending quality time with friends and family, or sometimes just to have a plain old good time. The motivating factor for a trip to the ballpark is as unique as the individuals who come to spend a summer night at the yard.

Being in my position, I'm often asked to speak publicly. These speeches can be as varied as the reasons that drive people to watch a baseball game. I've spoken to as many as a couple hundred people to as few as a handful. The groups range from school age kids to senior citizens. Some people are die-hard baseball fans and others don't know a thing about the sport. Thus, it becomes my mission to connect with the group and tailor my talk around them.

When I started the Round Rock Express in 1998, I was in high demand to give talks because minor league baseball was something new to the Central Texas area. It seemed like everywhere I went people wanted to hear about the fun of minor league baseball. Having played minor league baseball myself, my best personal story was about this crazy Italian guy named Dom Gatti.

As the story goes, Dom knew his playing career was nearing a close and he had secretly always wanted to get hit in the head by a pitch and run to third base (like I said, crazy Italian!). Well . . . you guessed it, opportunity knocked and Dom was at bat. The pitcher threw a ball up and in and sure enough, Dom got hit in the helmet right on the crown of his head.

The fans, not knowing Dom (or his intentions), were obviously very concerned. Dom put together an Oscar-winning performance and lamented on the ground, gripping his head and requesting smelling salts. Once he gave the manager, trainer and umpire (none of whom were in on the joke) the obligatory nod that he was okay, Dom promptly trotted to third base and stood with a stone cold poker face. Then, before anyone could act, he busted out the biggest smile, waved to the crowd and jogged across the infield to first base as our dugout rolled in laughter. It was a true *only-in-minor-league-baseball* moment.

As you can imagine, the groups that I spoke to all loved this story. The people left with the image of Dom in their heads, anxious to find this kind of fun at the ballgame.

This is the secret to delivering a great speech; understand what the audience wants to hear and then personalize the story for them. My story about Dom is one that small school children may not understand or a business group might find useless if they are looking for motivation. However, for baseball fans looking for affordable entertainment in their community, it hit the mark.

We all have stories. We have hundreds of stories. The key is finding the story that hits the mark with your audience. You don't need the voice of James Earl Jones or the presence of Tommy Lee Jones. All you have to do is give the audience what they want. One way to do that is with a personal story that reinforces why they came to see you speak. Oh yeah . . . and have some fun.

This is what Kevin Karschnik and Russ Peterson will teach you in this book. They have some fun and give you some great speaking tools along the way. It is the reason I have hired them to work with my staff. When learning is fun, it doesn't feel like learning at all. The same can be said for work and it can also be said for public speaking.

After reading *Corporate Ovations* you will approach every speech, presentation, or conversation differently because you will be focusing on your audience first. These tools apply to every speaking situation; whether you are speaking to a large audience, presenting to the board of directors, or even sharing stories with your buddies at a baseball game.

—REID RYAN, President and CEO, Ryan-Sanders Baseball,
Round Rock Express & Corpus Christi Hooks

Introduction

*"I alone cannot change the world,
but I can cast a stone across the waters
to create many ripples."*

—Mother Teresa, Humanitarian,
Winner, Nobel Peace Prize, 1979

Zig Ziglar was on stage at Palmer Auditorium in Austin, Texas. In his Southern drawl, with the words, "Let me tell you about a West Texas rancher . . . ," he moved into a story about motivation. The audience was captivated.

How did he do it? How did he motivate the audience so effortlessly? Why were thousands of attendees, including us, all glued to our seats?

Despite our years of experience presenting and teaching others how to present, it was in *that* moment, when we ourselves had been enraptured by a speaker, that we realized the need to build a formula and find an answer to an important question: What do great speakers do to captivate and motivate their audiences?

Of course, we had a pretty good feel for the other side of that coin. We were no strangers to bad presentations. In fact, we had certainly delivered a few duds of our own.

For example, early in our careers, there were a couple of instances where we did not confirm the size of the expected audience. In a sales presentation to a customer, Russ became mentally overwhelmed when the small conference-room audience he expected turned into one that filled a large auditorium. On another occasion, the opposite happened to Kevin. He was expecting 200 attendees for a seminar and ended up with only 22. In both cases we were able to deliver our presentations, but we had mental hurdles of either anxiety or disappointment that affected our ability to connect with the audience.

In another instance, we had arrived early for one of our workshops so we could have the room completely set up prior to our students' arrival. At the scheduled start time, everything was set up with curriculum, pens, handouts, and visual aids scrolling on the video screen as music played in the background. It was all going according to plan until we realized we were set up in the wrong room of the hotel. The students weren't running late … we were! This threw us into panic mode, which created a tremendous amount of anxiety for both of us. When we found the correct room, it was filled with concerned students. We then had to set up the room with the entire group watching. As a result of all of this, the workshop did not start off in a powerful way, and we weren't able to give our students the first impression we had planned.

Another area we both had to polish early in our careers was our stage movement. When Russ was asked to speak at a trade show in front of several hundred attendees, he did not take time to inspect the stage prior to his delivery. His movements took him to the back of the stage where he stepped off of the platform. As he began to fall he grabbed a large curtain to hold himself up. Luckily the entire structure didn't come down on top of him! After that, being aware of our surroundings and polishing our movements to have purpose became an area we knew we had to master.

With our past mistakes in mind, we reflected on our performances and compared them to those of more successful speakers: Tony Robbins' ability to make everyone in the audience feel like he had locked eyes with them, Brian Tracy's ability to access research studies in his mind in a split second, Zig Ziglar's ability to motivate others with his stories, and Les Brown's ability to connect with every audience. When we first started, both of us spoke to local clubs and organizations. Groups like the Sertoma Club, the Rotary Club, the Chamber of Commerce, or University Alumni groups are always looking for speakers. As we improved, our audiences became larger and included corporate names like DELL, Cameron, XO Communications, CenterPoint Energy, and Bimbo Bakeries.

From each presentation, we learned more. Over time, through observation, feedback, and reflection, we were able to extract the key ingredients for successful speaking. In your hands, you hold the results of our research and experience. This book contains the techniques and tools we learned—sometimes the hard way!—about what it takes to be a successful speaker.

We know these techniques and tools work, because after figuring out our formula, we tested it. The difference in our audiences' responses was amazing. We call our formula the nine-box model for presenting. The nine boxes are aligned in three rows of three. The first row is called *Prepare*. In this row you will study your subject and your audience. What do you need to *know* and what do you want your audience to *know?* What do you want them to *feel?* Finally what do you want them to *do* as a result of this presentation? The second row is called *Develop*. In this row, you will develop your presentation in three pieces, the *opening*, the *body*, and the *close*. The final row is called *Deliver*. In this row you will fine-tune the delivery of your presentation with the *visual*, *vocal* and *verbal* elements.

Since the development of our model, we've integrated the formula into our workshop curriculum. To date, we have taught our methods to thousands of students around the world. In our workshops, our students learn these techniques and have an opportunity to implement and practice their new skills. Each attendee is video recorded and receives personal feedback from us on their performances. Our coaching technique involves inspiring our students toward greatness through developmental feedback.

We always enjoy receiving comments from our students who are applying their new skills. The positive feedback we have received and the results we have heard from our students have been both exciting and humbling. We are happy to hear that these techniques are making a difference in the lives of many. It's truly amazing for us to hear that these communication tools have helped people not only at work, but also in their personal lives. We sincerely hope you can benefit from these methods throughout your life.

Sure, your next business presentation may not end in a standing ovation, but we do hope it ends in what we call a corporate ovation as participants give you positive feedback or praise after a job well done! The advice we provide in this book can get you those great results.

Satori

In each of our workshops, we introduce the group to a page in the back of their curriculum. The title at the top says *"Satori"* (Sah-tor-ee). It is a Japanese word that literally means *to understand.*

If you speak Japanese, you might argue that it is much more than understanding. In fact, it is a Zen Buddhist term that means *full enlightenment.* Now, our curriculum certainly doesn't bring our students full enlightenment (and unfortunately, this book won't either), but we hope our workshop curriculum brings them some "ah-ha" moments. So, in our workbooks, we always include pages labeled *"Satori"* so participants can capture these light-bulb moments. We hope sometime during the day they'll hear something and think, "Hmmm, that's good stuff. I could use that!" Writing these ideas in the workbook provides a record for future reference.

We hope you will have some *satori* moments while you are reading this book. So in the back, you will find several blank pages. These pages are for you to record all the light-bulb moments you have as you read. Think of it as a personal index. When you read something that sounds good or something you can use, we want you to turn to the *"Satori"* pages in the back and write it down. We also recommend you write down the page number for the topic. In the future, when you take this book down from your bookshelf (and we hope you do so frequently!), the *"Satori"* pages should be the first place you look. They're a great way to keep a record of everything that spoke to you in this book.

We invite you to not only read this book, but *to use* this book. Remember, nothing improves until something changes. So go get your pen or pencil and let's get started!

CHAPTER 1

Overcoming Fear and Anxiety

*"The human brain starts working the moment
you are born and it never stops
until you stand up to speak in public."*

—George Jessel, Actor and Producer

Anyone who has ever had to give a presentation knows the feeling. It's your turn to present. Suddenly, your heart rate increases. Your blood pressure rises. Your palms start to sweat. You feel something flittering about in your stomach, and you may even feel light headed! Why is this feeling so paralyzing? What is it about speaking in public that can turn an otherwise normal person into an absolute wreck? Well, that feeling is related to our human DNA and a common biological phenomenon called "fight or flight."

If you are ever scared for your life, your body responds by getting you ready to take on the challenge, or run away from the threat.[1] We certainly hope you are not scared for your life before a presentation, but when you're anxious about delivering it, your body tends to react in a similar fashion. Your heart rate increases. Your blood pressure escalates. Adrenalin is released into the body. You start to sweat. Endorphins are released in the brain. Synapses start to fire, causing acute focus.

All of this physiological change is taking place, right or wrong, because you are literally afraid to speak. Your body is in fight or flight mode. That funny feeling inside is excess energy. Your body is ready to release energy, but until you do, that energy will continue flying around inside you—usually in your stomach. This is where the term "butterflies in your stomach" comes from. As Art Linkletter noted, it's okay to have butterflies in your stomach. We just want them flying in formation.

As audience members, we've all seen and criticized some poor presentations. We know what we don't like, what works and what doesn't. Of course, there are some "usual suspects" ... the speaker reads from his slides. The speaker is monotone. The speaker looks nervous. The speaker did not take the time to customize the content to the audience. There are too many PowerPoint slides. The speaker never looks the audience in the eye. The list goes on and on. As a result, when we are the speaker, we start to focus on our audience being critical, and we can't help but become nervous and anxious!

> "Fear is part of being a speaker.
> You just have to get your butterflies
> flying in formation."[2]
>
> **—Art Linkletter**, Radio and Television Personality and Author

If you feel the pre-presentation fear, you're certainly not alone. In fact, what do you think Americans fear the most? It would have been great for this book if we could say public speaking, but alas ... it's not. It's actually snakes! However, when 1,016 adults were interviewed for a 2001 Gallop Poll, 40 percent *did* respond by saying public speaking was their greatest fear.[3]

You may have heard the joke that at a funeral, most people would rather be in the casket than delivering the eulogy! That's because studies consistently show that people fear public speaking more than they fear death. So, yeah, there's no denying that people have a real, persistent fear of speaking in public. But why?

In order to answer this, it's helpful to venture into the world of psychology and Maslow's hierarchy of needs.[4] (How far did you think we'd get into this book before we mentioned Maslow? We promise not to stay here long!) According to Maslow, one of our basic human needs is to feel accepted by a group. Based on his theory, it's obvious that speaking in public puts the need for group acceptance on trial.

Before a presentation, one starts to worry, *What if I speak in front of the group and they don't like me? What if they ask me a question and I don't know the answer? What if they discover that I'm not the most qualified to speak on this topic?* We all want to be accepted by others. We all feel loved when others make a big deal over us. Why do you think a surprise party makes a person feel so loved? It's because people have to go through tremendous toils to plan an event hidden from the guest of honor.

But when people do not accept us, we feel quite the opposite. We do not feel loved when others mock us, jeer at us or expose our flaws. Based on these facts about human nature, it becomes understandable why people will feel nervous about speaking in public . . . It all comes down to a common fear: *What if they don't accept me?*

> "Do the thing you fear
> and the death of fear is certain."
> **—Ralph Waldo Emerson,** Poet and Lecturer

Since we are not clinical psychologists, we won't spend any more time discussing why we feel fear or anxiety. Instead, let's all agree that regardless of the reason why, people tend to experience anxiety in varying degrees when they speak in public. We think the more important question on which to focus is, "What can we do to overcome this fear?" If we know we are going to experience the fear and anxiety of public speaking, we need to have a plan for overcoming that fear before it happens.

Here are a few things to keep in mind.

It's Okay to Feel Anxious

If you feel something moving around in your gut . . . that's good! It means you care. You care enough to want to do a good job for the audience. If you didn't feel anything, we'd question your intentions and motivation to present to your audience. In Texas, we have a saying about hanging up spurs. A cowboy who no longer rides his horse, no longer needs his spurs for his boots. So he hangs them up for good. As professional speakers, the day we don't feel anything before we take the stage is the day we hang up our spurs.

If you don't feel anything on the inside . . . maybe you no longer care. And if that is the case, you will be doing the audience a huge disservice by speaking without the passion they deserve to hear.

The Audience Wants You to Win

The audience truly wants you to win! What does that mean? It means that nobody wants to see a poor presentation. They want you to perform well. Just think about how you feel when you're about to watch a presentation? Are you hoping the speaker knocks it out of the park and delivers a riveting speech? Or are you hoping the speaker is so nervous he can't deliver a coherent thought? Most likely it's the former! For empathetic people, it's painful to see someone stammer, shake with nervousness, or freeze like the proverbial deer in the headlights. That's how your audiences feel too. Regardless of the topic or the situation, audiences want to see speakers succeed. They enjoy watching speakers who know how to deliver a message.

Now, some salespeople may disagree and say, "I've delivered presentations to some prospects in the past and they had already made up their mind to purchase from one of my competitors. Are you telling me that even that prospect wanted to see me win when I presented?" The answer is, "Yes, they *did* want to see you win . . . at presenting!" Even if they didn't plan on purchasing from you, the last thing they wanted to do was to sit in a boring presentation that put them to sleep! They wanted to see an enjoyable presentation.

Just knowing that the audience truly wants to see you succeed can reduce your anxiety level. Let that thought give you the energy to prepare effectively and give them what they want.

Know Your Subject

This may seem obvious, but you would be surprised how important it is when it comes to reducing your anxiety. As you become more comfortable with the subject matter, you become more relaxed during your presentation. When your mind is not concentrating on the content, it is freed to be creative. The creativity of the mind will take over your body language and begin to align your physical delivery with your message.

Keep in mind, though, that your goal is not to be the smartest person in the room. Speaking is not an IQ test. You were asked to speak because your delivery and insights are viewed as valuable to this particular audience. Too many novice speakers will focus on their knowledge of the subject when preparing. Then they feel anxiety when they find out that someone in the audience may know more than them.

Don't let that distract you. Assume someone will always know more than you and understand that that is okay. You were asked to speak because you are able to communicate your ideas. Focus on that fact.

We're sure you have attended presentations where the speaker was extremely knowledgeable, maybe even the smartest person in the room, but they were ineffective in delivering their message because of their inability to communicate effectively. While you don't need to be the smartest person in the room, you do need to know your subject and to have the ability to present that knowledge in a way that really captures your audience.

Prepare for Tough Questions

When we ask our students about their greatest fears prior to one of their speaking engagements, many of them say they are afraid that someone will ask them a question and they won't have an answer. Our response is always, "So what?" Seriously, what if you don't know the answer? We will discuss in detail in Chapter Eleven how to handle situations where you don't have an appropriate response to a question. For now, let's focus on what you can do to prepare for those tough questions.

Assume that you will always have a tough audience. Next, assume that the audience will ask you the absolute toughest questions possible. Now, make a list of those tough questions. It will do you no good to make a list of the tough questions and then say to yourself, "Well . . . let's hope they don't ask these!" Once you have a list of tough questions, then comes the hard part . . . coming up with the answers! Prepare answers to these potentially tough questions and rehearse your response to each. It can even be helpful to role-play these with a friend so that you can get their feedback on your answer, your body language and your vocal delivery.

Rehearse Your Delivery

This is one of the toughest things to do because it takes time, and time is the resource most of us have too little of already. You have to get your priorities in order. If you do not place a high priority on your presentation, you will make every excuse not to rehearse. You must be honest with yourself and ask, "How important is my delivery of this presentation?"

Effective presentation deliveries do not happen by accident. Author and speaker Lilly Walters says, "Stage fright can be reduced by 75 percent through simple preparation and rehearsal."[5] If you are truly interested in a great delivery, you must find the time to rehearse.

So how exactly should you go about rehearsal? Is there some kind of a process to follow? Yes! We have found an effective methodology for rehearsal. It's a process that can be customized depending on the presentation you are delivering, the audience, and the time you are given to present. In Chapter Twelve, we will discuss rehearsal and evaluation of your presentation in more detail.

For now, here's an overview: Start by just reading your presentation several times. After you have read the presentation several times, read it out loud several more times focusing especially on the opening and the close. As you read it out loud, listen carefully to how you are emphasizing certain words, how you are using pauses after questions, and how you are using the inflections in your voice.

After you have delivered it out loud several times, stand and deliver your presentation in front of a live audience (your peers, your friends, your spouse, your children, etc). It is also helpful to record yourself with a video camera. If you do not have the time to record a full presentation, deliver and record only the key elements. The key elements will include the opening, the close and the main points in the body of the presentation. Once you have recorded the delivery, spend some time evaluating your performance and making adjustments.

> "Do the thing you fear . . . that is the quickest and surest way ever yet discovered to conquer fear."[6]
> —**Dale Carnegie,** Speaker, Teacher, and Author of
> *The Quick and Easy Way to Effective Speaking*

Arrive Early

On the day of your presentation, plan on arriving early. Early arrival allows you to set up and test any audio/visual equipment, meet attendees, lay out your materials, and walk the area where you will be speaking.

Whenever we arrive early for a speaking engagement, we make every effort to meet some of the attendees. After casual conversation with these people, we usually ask them several questions, "Why are you attending today? What are your thoughts on *(topic of the day)*? Where will you be sitting today?" Getting this information is great because it can help you customize your presentation. In addition to customization, if you have a large audience and you know where the people you've met will be sitting, you can always look to them to make eye contact with a friendly face. Don't underestimate the calming effect on the nerves when you flash a smile at an audience member and they smile back!

Regardless of how you fill your time when you arrive early, it's worth it. If you are in a rush prior to speaking, you will definitely not be relaxed . . . and it will show!

Walk Around

As we stated in our discussion of fight or flight, the butterflies we feel in our stomach come from excess energy. That energy needs someplace to go. As Einstein clarified for us, energy is never lost, only transferred[7]. With this principle in mind, the best use of the energy inside our nervous stomachs is to transfer it . . . to the audience!

We have all seen speakers who are nervous and as they continue to speak and bottle up the nervous energy inside them, they actually seem to inflate. Their shoulders begin to move back while their chin lifts up. Their chest seems to get larger as they inflate with the energy bottled up inside them. Nobody touch the speaker, he might pop!

Energy can work to your detriment if you do not release it properly. For those speakers who have extra energy inside them, we always recommend movement prior to a presentation.

For example, when Russ visits a high-rise building downtown to deliver a presentation in a conference room, he will often ask, "Which way is the restroom?" A typical response is, "Oh, it's down the hall to the left and you will see it." Most buildings in a downtown setting are arranged with each floor in a large loop. Instead of returning directly to the conference room, Russ will take a lap around the entire floor to release excess energy through his legs. We don't recommend jogging laps around the office, but a quick walk outside the conference room can do the trick.

If you still have energy bottled up inside when you begin the presentation, we recommend you transfer that energy to the audience. Doing so can be as simple as raising your voice as you speak, adding a sweeping hand gesture, or talking faster. Energy transferred to the audience will energize them. Keep in mind that the energy you bring to a presentation is contagious. In many cases, your audience will return the favor by transferring energy back to you with either laughter or applause. There are many other methods to transfer energy to your audience with your body language and your vocals. We will share more techniques on delivering energy to your audience in Chapters Eight and Nine.

Take Three Deep Breaths

With an increased heart rate and higher blood pressure, calming yourself can be as simple as taking three deep cleansing breaths. The best way to take relaxing breaths is to inhale a deep breath through the nose, hold it for two seconds, and then release it through the mouth. Doing this three times can have an amazing relaxing effect on you.

We mentioned this in one of our workshops and a woman in the back row raised her hand and said, "We do that in my yoga class."

We asked, "Why do you do that in yoga?" The woman replied, "It's a form of relaxation. We do it to center ourselves and meditate. It calms your body and relaxes your mind." We responded by saying, "That's why professional speakers do it too!"

In his audio book, *Breathing: The Master Key to Self-Healing*[8], Dr. Andrew Weil describes these three in-and-out breath cycles as stimulating breaths, which are adapted from a yogic breathing technique. Three deep breaths can work within seconds and have a profound effect on your energy, and how your audience perceives you. However, we do recommend that you take these deep breaths *before* you take the stage!

> "Breathing control gives a person strength, vitality, inspiration and magic powers."[9]
>
> —**Chuang Tzu**, Chinese Philosopher

Have a Drink

Wait, wait, it's not what you think! As much as some may want to interpret this method as taking a shot of so-called liquid courage, that is not what we mean. We do, however, recommend drinking some warm water or tea.

For many people, soup and hot tea are comfort foods. How do they make you feel on the inside? Chances are that the warm tea or soup give you a warm-fuzzy feeling in your stomach and have a calming effect on you. Warm liquids tend to do that to us.

If you want to calm your nerves a bit, we recommend a trick that many professional speakers use. Have warm water with a twist of lemon or a shot of honey before your presentation. This warm concoction will have a tremendous calming effect on your stomach and your nerves. In addition, it warms the throat to prepare it for action. Even the Mayo Clinic[10] recommends caffeine-free tea or warm water with honey to soothe your throat.

On the other hand, ice cold, carbonated drinks are the worst things you can drink before speaking. They tighten the throat, don't relieve stress, and give you gas. We think you'll agree, that's not a pretty picture. Of course we would definitely recommend an ice-cold, refreshing Coke to celebrate *after* your presentation.

Try to avoid too much warm coffee or tea because of the caffeine. Even for those who say, "Caffeine really doesn't affect me much," we recommend you let others be the judge of that. Caffeine affects all people, some more than others, but it affects all people. If caffeine makes your hands shake, your audience will interpret it to mean that you are nervous, even if you're not.

Know that everyone who takes the stage feels the energy on the inside. Professionals know how to control and use the energy to their advantage. Amateurs will allow the energy to take over the delivery and leak out through nervous voice, hands, and movements. Take control of your presentations and expect those energizing butterflies to show up. Then, be prepared to harness and control that energy.

────────── **CHAPTER HIGHLIGHTS** ──────────

- It's perfectly normal to be nervous before delivering a presentation. Anxiety is part of being a good speaker; the key is to not allow it to distract the audience from your message. As Art Linkletter said, *"You just have to get your butterflies flying in formation."*

- Feeling anxious means you care enough to want to do a good job for your audience.

- Audiences truly want you to win! Regardless of the topic or the situation, audiences want to watch a speaker who knows how to deliver an engaging message.

- There are seven methods for overcoming fear and anxiety:
  › Know your subject.
  › Prepare for tough questions.
  › Take time to rehearse.
  › Arrive early.
  › Walk around.
  › Take three deep breaths.
  › Have a drink.

────────── **TOMORROW'S CHALLENGE** ──────────

As you prepare for your next presentation, answer these questions:

☐ Are you nervous prior to presenting? Why?

☐ What are your audience's perceptions of you and your topic?

☐ Which of the methods for overcoming anxiety can you apply?

CHAPTER 2

Know Your Purpose

*"If you don't know where you're going,
you'll probably end up someplace else."*

—Yogi Berra, Hall of Fame Catcher
New York Yankees

Be selfish for a moment. That's right, think only about yourself and answer the following question: What do you want to accomplish through your presentations? Or try a simpler way of asking that question, "Why?" Why are you going to speak to the audience?

When you start to prepare for a presentation, "Why?" is the most important question. If you can't answer why you will speak to a group then you can put this book down and save yourself some time. Before you begin the construction of any speech or presentation, you need a defined destination or goal. You need a purpose. Without a purpose, speeches will wander around the information until they eventually come to an end, leaving the audience to wonder, "What was the point of all that?"

Some call this a selfish question because it focuses on the speaker instead of the audience. What do *you* want to accomplish by giving this presentation? While it may seem selfish on the surface, it is really quite the opposite. If you have no idea why you are speaking to this group, then the audience will not receive what they came for either. *Corporate Ovations* come from audiences who receive a gift from the speaker. And while we may jest about being selfish when identifying your purpose and goal, don't ever forget, in the end, it's really all about the audience!

> "When you fail to prepare,
> you are preparing to fail."[1]
> **—Coach John Wooden,**
> Hall of Fame NCAA Basketball Coach

Three Types of Presentations

To best understand how to define the purpose of your speech, you must first determine the type of presentation you are giving. Presentations come in three varieties: persuasive, informative, and entertaining. Once you know the type of presentation you are delivering, the purpose is easier to define.

> "Expect the best, plan for the worst,
> and prepare to be surprised."[2]
> **—Denis Waitley,**
> Motivational Speaker and Best-selling Author

At first glance, it may appear that your presentations are actually a combination of all three types. We can hear some of you right now, "Yep, mine are all three! I deliver a lot of information to my prospective customers. Then, I need to persuade them to buy from me. And, I always like to incorporate humor in my presentations."

That may appear to be true; however, judging by the statement above, the presentation is persuasive, because the desired end result requires persuasion to "Buy from me!" And if that's the case, the desired result is not to inform or entertain. When anything persuasive enters the mix, it trumps the other two! Really, you could make the argument that most presentations are classified as persuasive.

Ralph Waldo Emerson, American essayist, lecturer, and poet said, "Speech is power: speech is to persuade, to convert, to compel." Every great speaker needs to be motivational and engaging, while maintaining the ability to convey solid material that is credible, applicable, and flexible.[3]

So why is it so important to understand which type of presentation you will be delivering? Because your ultimate goal or purpose (whether it's to persuade, inform or entertain) will be your target as you develop your presentation. In addition, your purpose will also be tied directly to a portion of your closing remarks, which we will cover later in Chapter Five.

> "You persuade a man only insofar as
> you can talk his language by speech,
> gesture, tonality, order, image, attitude,
> idea, identifying your ways with his."
>
> **—Kenneth Burke,** Philosopher

Persuasive Presentations

If your goal is to convince the audience to take action, your presentation type is called persuasive. Persuasive presentations can make their request through logical appeals to the mind, emotional appeals to the heart, or both. But in most business cases, persuasion will rely more heavily on the logical appeal to the mind.

Constructing a presentation by building a case through logical arguments will show the requested action as the only logical alternative for the audience. Dr. Leon Festinger and other social psychologists call this cognitive dissonance.[4] People have a motivational drive to reduce their dissonance by making changes to their existing conditions.

When done effectively, however, appealing to the heart on an emotional level can also create the necessary desire to make a change. Non-profit organizations soliciting donations for a worthy cause serve as good examples for speakers who are looking for effective ways to use emotions to persuade their audiences.

For certain goals, making an emotional appeal is, indeed, much more effective than choosing to persuade with solely a logical argument. This is why an eight-year-old girl selling cookies to raise money can persuade you to buy cookies, whether you want them or not! Jan Gunter, Communications Manager at Ronald McDonald House Charities, uses family stories to inspire her audiences to maintain hope. Another example is television commercials pleading for donations to support a cause. They will always contain pictures and stories of people who have been affected. These emotional appeals can be quite powerful.

Here are a few more examples of purposes that would require the creation of a persuasive-style speech.

Sales Presentation Purpose
My goal is to persuade the prospect to agree we have a viable option. I want them to approve our next step to gather data from their IT department so we can create a proposal for services.

Purpose from a Non-Profit Soliciting a Donation
My purpose is to compel the audience to make a donation to support our cause.

Senior Manager Requesting Approval on Her Budget
I need to convince senior management that the projects planned for this coming year will be a benefit not only to my group, but to

the entire organization. As a result, I will get their verbal approval on my budget.

Project Manager Seeking Approval to Move Forward on the Project
My goal is to gain the approval of the senior management to proceed to the next phase of our project.

> "We succeed only as we identify a single overriding objective, and make all other considerations bend to that one objective."
> **—Dwight D. Eisenhower,**
> Former President of the United States

Informative Presentations

As a speaker, there may be times when there is no immediate requested action from the audience. They just need to learn and understand your topic. Of course, your hope is always that they will take their newfound knowledge and implement what they have learned to make a positive change in their life. However, your *immediate* goal is only to have the audience fully comprehend your presentation topic.

For example, Keith Dyer, executive director at the Texas Baptist Children's Home and one of our students, has to provide a quarterly update to the board of directors. He explains the financial statements for the quarter and the implications of those numbers to the organization. That's it. He delivers the information they need, and at least where those presentations are concerned, that's all they want from him.

When giving an information-driven presentation, while you may not require any specific actions from the audience, you do want to know that they have been informed and they understand the material.

Here are a few examples of presentation purposes for informative presentations:

Manager Providing an Update to his Team on Production Levels
My purpose is to inform the team of our current production levels since the implementation of the new production process.

Trainer delivering a presentation on the new process for entering data in to a system
I will educate the audience to a level of understanding and skill on the new data entry process.

Project Manager delivering an update on the project status
I will provide a project status including all our milestones and all of our current setbacks.

Teacher explaining the method for performing long division by hand
My objective is to educate the students on the importance of learning long division by hand. I will also educate them on the appropriate process for performing long division.

> "I went to a bookstore and asked the saleswoman,
> 'Where's the self-help section?'
> She said if she told me, it would defeat the purpose."
> —**George Carlin,** Comedian and Actor

Entertaining Presentations

If the end goal of the presentation is strictly entertainment, then the presentation is classified as "entertaining." There is no action to be taken and there is nothing to learn ... it's just meant to entertain.

While it is desirable to have elements of entertainment in all presentations, those elements do not classify your presentation as strictly entertaining. Usually, your presentation will have some other greater purpose. Elements of entertainment are just used to get the attention of the audience so you can zero them in on your main purpose.

"Entertaining" presentations have no grander purpose. They're strictly meant to entertain. That's it. Bill Cosby[5] and Jerry Seinfeld[6] deliver entertaining presentations. They have one goal and one goal only … to entertain their audiences. Professional entertainers often deliver these types of presentations. The purpose of the entertainer is always going to be the same, regardless of the situation. The purpose is to entertain the audience. By definition, entertaining presentations are fun to deliver but not necessarily easy to develop. It is much harder than it looks, but professionals like Billy Crystal make it look easy.

Here are a few appropriate scenarios for using an entertaining presentation:

A Professional Keynote Speaker Delivering the Message at the Sales Awards Dinner
I will entertain the audience.

A Comedian Speaking on Stage at a Comedy Club
I will entertain the audience.

Senior Manager Delivering a Farewell Speech to a Colleague Who is Retiring
I will entertain the audience.

> "Management is about persuading people
> to do things they do not want to do,
> while leadership is about inspiring people
> to do things they never thought they could."
> —**Steve Jobs**, Co-Founder of Apple

Know/Feel/Do

Once you have determined what type of presentation you are delivering, the Know/Feel/Do method can help you crystallize your purpose. This method is completed by asking yourself three questions:

1. What do you want your audience to know?
2. What do you want them to feel?
3. What do you want them to do?

For example, if you are presenting your annual budget to upper management to gain their approval, you might answer these questions with the following responses:

What Do You Want Them to Know?

I want upper management to understand we have cut our expenses in software and support by 20 percent. Therefore, if we had not managed our changes properly this past year, the increase in budget of 6 percent would have been 26 percent. I also want them to know the additional equipment will provide less downtime for our servers, which means productivity increases for the entire company.

What Do You Want Them to Feel?

I want them to trust our department and how we approach our budget with the overall company in mind.

What Do You Want Them to Do?

I want them to verbally approve my budget in the meeting so I can begin planning.

When you answer these three questions, you have documented your reason for speaking. Now you have a target.

"The measure of a great teacher isn't what he or
she knows; it's what the students know."
—**John C. Maxwell,** Leadership Expert,
Speaker, Coach, and Author

Know Where You're Going

Having coached thousands of individuals, we are often asked, "Is it really necessary to take the time to write a purpose for my presentation?" The short answer is, "Absolutely!"

Here's why. Picture this . . . the next time you finish delivering a presentation, we look you straight in the eye and ask you one very simple and direct question, "Did you achieve what you wanted to achieve with that presentation?" Before you answer, we need to caution you that there are only two acceptable answers to the question . . . You can either answer with "Yes, I did." Or you can answer with "No, I did not." Those are the only two acceptable answers!

Of course, we want to hear that you *did* achieve your objective. Unacceptable answers are "Yeah . . . I think so." Or "Maybe . . . I guess we will have to wait and see." To us, these answers are the same as saying, "No, I did not." You either did or you didn't. There is no maybe when it comes to achieving the purpose of your presentation. We want certainty, and more importantly, so does your audience.

"Luck is what happens
when preparation meets opportunity."
—**Seneca,** Roman Stoic Philosopher

—————————— **CHAPTER HIGHLIGHTS** ——————————

- The most important question to ask yourself before writing your presentation is, "What is the purpose of my presentation?"
- Presentations come in three varieties:
  › Persuasive
  › Informative
  › Entertaining
- You should be able to identify specifically what your audience should Know, Feel, and Do at the conclusion of your presentation.

—————————— **TOMORROW'S CHALLENGE** ——————————

As you prepare for your next presentation, answer these questions:

- ☐ Why have I been asked to deliver this presentation?
- ☐ What type of presentation will I be developing (Persuasive, Informative, or Entertaining)?
- ☐ What do I want my audience to Know, Feel, and Do at the conclusion of my presentation?

CHAPTER 3

Audiences Want You to Connect

"Connecting with people begins with knowing people. If you don't have clarity concerning your listeners, your message will be muddy."

—John C. Maxwell, Leadership Expert, Speaker, Coach, and Author

In the previous chapter, we asked you to be a little selfish and think only of what *you* wanted to get out of your presentation. But now that you have defined its purpose . . . it's time to re-focus on the folks who really matter—your audience!

We've all seen speakers before who seem to speak intelligently on their topic, but have absolutely no connection with the audience. These speakers may be highly educated in their subject matter. They may have amazing experiences of struggle and success, have lived through incredible adventures or overcome fantastic obstacles in life. Or they may be highly skilled at their craft, like a professional athlete, successful entrepreneur or a renowned artist. Audiences may show up for these types of speakers, but they will quickly zone out if the speaker doesn't make any effort to connect with them.

Speakers connect with audiences by serving them. And you serve your audience best by preparing a great presentation and by ensuring that your presentation will provide value to them.

> "I try to bring the audience's own drama—
> tears and laughter they know about—to them."
> —**Judy Garland**, Actress and Singer

Proper preparation for speaking takes place in three key areas: your subject matter, your audience and your purpose. Each of these three areas is important to delivering a high value presentation to the audience. In Chapter Two we reviewed the importance of knowing your purpose for speaking, and this chapter deals with knowing the audience.

As John Maxwell wrote in his book *Everyone Communicates, Few Connect*, "Anytime you aren't sure about how to bridge the communication gap, don't start the process by telling people about yourself. Begin with moving to where they are and seeing things from their perspective. Adapt to them—don't expect them to adapt to you."[1]

Know Your Subject

Have you ever attended an event to hear a speaker and after the presentation ended, you couldn't recall one significant piece of information delivered? If a speaker does not prepare her subject matter properly, the audience will not retain the true meaning of the information.

Too many individuals think that they have been delivering presentations on a specific topic for so long that there is no need to prepare. Not so! Even if a speaker is the most knowledgeable person in the world on that topic, if she doesn't take the time to structure her message to align with the needs of the audience, she won't connect with them. Her message will fall upon deaf ears.

Don't try to be perfect. Try to be effective.

You can probably recall some teachers or college professors you had who were extremely knowledgeable on their topic. You know, like the ones who had actually written the textbook you were using in the class! But you may also remember the many lectures when you and your fellow classmates struggled to stay awake as the professor dryly cycled through his PowerPoint slides.

Of course, it is important to understand your subject matter before speaking, but your knowledge is not the only focus for preparation. As the college professor example illustrates, you can be the smartest person in the room on a topic and not deliver an effective presentation. The professor may have gotten all of the information right, but members of the class struggled to come away with what they needed.

When delivering a presentation, your goal is not to be perfect; it's to be effective. And the good news is you don't have to be the smartest person in the room on a topic to deliver an effective presentation. (Was that a collective sigh of relief we just heard?) You simply have to know your subject well enough to convey your message to the audience and then have the ability to deliver that message with confidence.[2]

Sir Ken Robinson, one of the world's leading speakers, shares a story of a little girl in art class who never paid attention to her teacher. One day the teacher noticed she was listening attentively during the art lesson. The teacher walked over to see what she was drawing and she asked the little girl, "What are you drawing?" The girl said, "I'm drawing a picture of God." The teacher said, "Well, you can't do that. Nobody knows what God looks like." To which the little girl replied, "Well, they will in a minute." The lesson? You may not have the answer to everything, but if you are able to deliver your interpretation of the material with confidence, the audience will follow.[3]

> "If you're not prepared to be wrong,
> you'll never come up with anything creative."
> —**Sir Ken Robinson,** Teacher on Innovation and Author

Some argue the message is more important than delivery. For example, if a medical research scientist took the stage and announced an absolute cure for cancer, the audience response would be a standing ovation, regardless of the scientist's ability to present effectively. While it makes sense that the message is much more important than the delivery in this example, most of our presentations on weekly sales figures or project updates don't always elicit the same level of admiration from our audiences.

When it comes to message and delivery, we believe the two work best together. We will focus later on your delivery methods using voice and body language. But for now, let's take a look at how to tailor your presentation to your audience.

Know Your Audience

Recently, we both attended the Chick-fil-A Leadercast Conference[4] to hear a group of experts speak on the topic of leadership. Some of the speakers had a definite connection with the audience. For these speakers, there was a feeling of energy being transferred from them to the audience as they gave valuable insights into the topic. The audience would then return the energy with laughter and applause.

While most of the speakers were great, there were a few who just weren't able to make the same kind of connection with the audience. Why is that? It's because the great speakers knew what the audience wanted and used that information to prepare a message tailored specifically to them. Professional speakers will tell you that the time they feel most alive is when they are on stage, truly connecting with an audience.[5]

It's not what you say that's important,
it's what they hear.

Imagine an IT presentation from a software engineer meant to persuade a customer to buy their technology. First, the engineer prepares a presentation to deliver to engineers at the customer's site. The group of engineers loves the technology and approves the project from a technical standpoint. Then, the customer's executive team is notified of the engineering team's selection.

The executives at the customer site ask to have the solution presented to them the following week before they will give financial approval. Unfortunately, the sales engineer does not have the foresight to adjust the presentation to the new executive audience. As a result, the engineer consistently speaks with too much technical jargon and detail. Within 15 minutes of the hour-long presentation, the executives are no longer listening, and as a result, the software company does not win the business.

If the message is not prepared specifically for the audience, it will not hit the target. When an audience attends a given presentation, they obviously want something. They are constantly asking themselves, "What's in it for me?" Steve Jobs was the master at answering that question for his audiences. He had a special ability to connect the dots between what he wanted them to know and why they needed to care. In the audience analysis, it is important to identify what the audience is going to expect—information, persuasion or entertainment. Only by identifying their expectations will you be able to identify what you should offer to them.

> "The success of your presentation will be judged not by the knowledge you send but by what the listener receives."[6]
>
> —**Lilly Walters,** Professional Speaker and
> Co-Author of *Speak and Grow Rich*

Align Your Purpose and Audience

Some of you may have seen JC Anderson's short instructional video on how to properly swing a golf club.[7] He begins speaking at a very fast pace using extremely technical words and jargon to describe the geometry of the circle and the physics of the muscular thrust required in a two-line delivery path. His technical explanation goes on for over a minute and upon completion he moves into a demonstration. As he strikes the golf ball it bounces straight up in the air to his hand, to which he acts completely surprised. He quickly throws the ball forward and fakes a completed swing.

JC Anderson's Golf Lesson
http://www.CorporateOvations.com/golflesson

The first question we would ask is, "Did JC achieve his purpose?" Most will want to immediately answer, "No, he didn't," but don't answer yet, because it is a trick question. You don't know what his purpose was!

So, what if we told you his presentation is informative and his purpose was to educate you on how to properly swing a golf club. Now answer, did he achieve his purpose? Gotcha! It is another trick question. You can't answer until you ask about his audience. If we tell you he was speaking to you and me, average weekend golfers, now you can answer the question, "Did he achieve his purpose?" No, he did not achieve his purpose. Most of us are more confused now than before he began his explanation!

Now, let's change the scenario. Let's assume JC is trying to inform his audience on how to swing a golf club better, and his audience is a group of physicists from MIT. Now tell us, did JC achieve his purpose? With that type of explanation to that type of audience, he may have actually achieved his goal to inform the audience on swinging the golf club. The answer is now a definite maybe.

Let's change the scenario one more time. Let's now assume the audience is back to you and me, the average golfer. This time, let's change his purpose from an informative presentation to an entertaining presentation. In other words, his sole purpose and goal is to entertain his audience. Now answer the question, "Did he achieve his purpose?" While the video may not be hilarious, it was definitely entertaining. Yes, JC did achieve his purpose.

Audiences know when you are
speaking to yesterday's audience.

The golf video is a great example because it shows how just changing the purpose or the audience of a presentation can change its success rate. By changing one or both elements, a presentation can go from a miserable failure to a *Corporate Ovation*! Make certain you properly define your purpose and your audience before constructing your presentations. It is the only way to know if you have achieved success.

────────── **CHAPTER HIGHLIGHTS** ──────────

- If you don't take the time to customize and prepare your message, you set yourself up for failure.

- It is equally important to know your subject and connect with the audience.

- *Corporate Ovations* occur when the speaker aligns their presentation purpose with the audience's needs.

────────── **TOMORROW'S CHALLENGE** ──────────

As you prepare for your next presentation, answer these questions:

- ☐ How will I connect with my audience?
- ☐ What does my audience need to know?
- ☐ How can my audience relate to me or my topic?

CHAPTER 4

Open with Power

"Politics is just like show business—
you have a great opening, you coast for awhile,
you have a great close."

—Ronald Reagan,
Former President of the United States

The scene opens with a crowded mob of rough-looking gamblers placing bets on either a king cobra or a mongoose as they face off in the pit. Mingled in with the crowd is a man who is obviously not a local and looks somewhat out of place as he talks on an earpiece communicator to a colleague. As the camera pans beyond the crowd of rabid fans, the focus turns upward to another man leaning against a wall on a second story elevation. It's the colleague on the other end of the earpiece communicator: James Bond.

Both men are monitoring one gambler in the crowd who receives a text message and then begins to hastily exit the crowd for an obviously more important task. As the thief moves through the crowd toward Bond's secret agent accomplice, the thief becomes suspicious as he notices how this local tourist is obviously out of place. After all, what local tourist would ever use an earpiece communicator? With an awkward lock of the eyes between the two men, the chase begins!

For almost 10 minutes the movie audience is treated to aerial stunts, multiple explosions, hand-to-hand combat, gunshots, obstacles, maneuvers, and ultimately, James Bond getting his man. That is how *Casino Royale* introduces the newest actor to play the infamous James Bond, Daniel Craig . . . and he doesn't disappoint loyal Bond fans.

Casino Royale Opening Action Sequence
http://www.CorporateOvations.com/casinoroyale

With every James Bond movie you know you are going to get one thing for sure—a great opening action scene! A memorable opening is a standard formula for stories, television shows, movies and plays. Writers know that they must capture the attention of the audience from the very start. It doesn't always have to be an action sequence either. For example, with a murder mystery, the opening sequence could be a chalk outline on the floor of a crime scene. For a love story, we might be introduced to the lonely world of the main character before he meets that special someone.

We know that speaking to our audiences in a corporate environment may not be as exhilarating as James Bond jumping off a construction crane from ten stories in the sky, but we can still learn a lesson. From the very start, audiences need to know they will get something out of a presentation. As a speaker, your challenge is to capture their attention and let them know your delivery has been customized with their needs in mind.

Some Fortune 500 corporations like Cisco Systems record anonymous feedback from audience members after their executives speak.[1] They want to gather the information so the executives can continue to improve their speaking abilities. And as representatives for the entire company, they welcome the opportunity to improve. CEO of Cisco, John Chambers' reputation as an engaging and dynamic speaker proves the company's dedication to improving based on audience feedback is paying off.

> "We don't know where
> our first impressions come from,
> or precisely what they mean,
> so we don't always appreciate their fragility."
>
> —**Malcolm Gladwell,** Author of *Blink,*
> *The Tipping Point* and *Outliers*

First Impressions Set the Tone

You know your purpose for speaking and you have analyzed your audience. Using these two elements as your foundation, you must now ask yourself another question, "What can I do or say from the very start to capture my audience's attention and connect with them?" When you take the stage your audience will collect enough information in a few seconds to create a first impression of you and your presentation.

In his book *Blink: The Power of Thinking without Thinking*[2], Malcolm Gladwell suggests that we make snap judgments based on our knowledge and past experiences without even thinking. He refers to this as "thin-slicing." We do it so that we can make decisions in the blink of an eye. Many people understand we are susceptible to making snap decisions without thinking. But as we gather more data, we have the ability to change our impression. So the good news is that the first impression does not have to be the lasting impression.

Understand that you will be evaluated from the very start of your presentation. Practically before you even open your mouth, a lot of audiences can evaluate your level of confidence and how receptive or tuned-in you are to the audience. After the initial impression is formed in the first few seconds, some audience members will actually decide whether they will actively listen to you or only passively listen while they check their email, daydream or count the ceiling tiles. Knowing that the entire audience will evaluate you from the very start, you need to put special focus on how you open your presentation.

Let's take a look at a speech opening we've probably all heard at least once:

> "Ladies and gentlemen, thank you for coming today. My name is John Houser and for those of you who don't know me, I'm the Director of Marketing for our Southwest Region. Dave asked me to speak to you guys today and share a little history on what we've been doing in our region to overcome the slow demand we've all experienced since the end of last year. So, let's get started . . ."

Sounds familiar, right? Many corporate presentations probably open a little like that. Is there anything wrong with that opening? No, there's not necessarily anything wrong with it, but we would argue it could be improved. In fact, we think two critical pieces are missing. First, there was nothing in that opening to grab the audience's attention or to pique their interest. Second, the speaker didn't tell the audience what was in it for them—he didn't connect. In other words, what will the audience get out of this presentation? Why should the audience keep listening?

> "You can have brilliant ideas, but if you can't get them across, your ideas won't get you anywhere."
> —**Lee Iacocca**, Former CEO of Chrysler and Author

The CABA Formula

The formula we use for opening a presentation includes four key elements: Credibility, Attention, Body, and Audience (CABA). When all four pieces are delivered to the audience, you capture the listeners from the very beginning. These four pieces can be delivered to the audience in any order. The sequence used depends on the speaker's preference, the purpose, and the audience. You cannot make a strong case with the content in the body of your presentation if the audience is checked out and not listening. Give your audiences the corporate version of a James Bond movie opening.

The four ingredients of CABA
(Credibility, Attention, Body, and Audience)
can be delivered to the audience in any order.

First, let's learn more about CABA:

Credibility

The audience wants to know why *you* are speaking on this topic. Why are you the trusted source for this information? What knowledge or experience do you have that uniquely qualifies you as the speaker on this topic?

Too often we hear speakers fulfill this part of the formula with something like, "My name is Russel Boles and I've been practicing law for over 14 years."[3] We caution our students from using only the quantity of years to legitimize their credibility. First of all, just because you've been doing something for 14 years doesn't mean you ever got it right! And secondly, that method tends to get overused. When you start out with the same boring line that they heard at the last presentation they saw, your audience will imme-diately equate you with that boring speaker.

Instead, tell your audience why you are uniquely qualified to speak on the topic of the day. A revised introduction for Mr. Boles might sound like this:

> My name is Russel Boles and I've been selling commercial real estate and practicing law for over 14 years. Not only can I assist my clients in finding the right property, I can review purchase contracts, facilitate zoning matters, and handle entitlement issues on their behalf.
>
> When I was in Georgetown last week to meet with Jim, our CEO, he shared his insights on the future of our Central Texas region.

With a statement like this, the audience has received the reason why Russel is going to share the vision for the future of the Central Texas region. He met with the CEO and discussed the future of the region. Now he is going to share those insights with the audience. There is only one other person uniquely qualified to deliver this message to this audience and that would be Jim, the CEO.

Now, let's try another:

> "For the past two weeks, I've served on the internal audit team with the primary focus of reviewing our travel expenses. During that time, I noticed three distinct trends since the beginning of this year."

In this example, the audience may already know you as the presenter. In fact, they may all have worked with you for over three years now, but your credibility must still be established for the topic you are sharing. Since you have been working on a special project you will make your audience aware of what you have been focusing on over the past two weeks. This shows your colleagues that you have an insight and you are uniquely qualified to share some new information with them.

How about one more?

> My name is Sarah Benwick, and I'm the Chief Learning Officer for Ascendant Aerospace. My experience in Learning & Development includes three years in public education as a high school principal, seven years as a school superintendent, and four years as a Lead Consultant in corporate learning and development for Fortune 500 customers. In each of these roles, I've noticed how the success of the learner has always been tied to a mentor who took an interest in the development of the student.

If you are speaking to a large audience unfamiliar with you or your background, it is helpful to provide this kind of abbreviated resume information to establish your credibility. But in addition to the biographical information, did you notice how Sarah included one sentence on what she learned along the way? That one sentence helps her make the transition from her credibility statement to her topic for the day. It also sets her up to segue nicely into what the audience will gain from listening to her, which she can accomplish with a simple statement like, "Today I will share with you the four necessary ingredients for an effective mentoring program."

> "Human behavior flows from three main sources: desire, emotion and knowledge."
> —**Plato**, Greek Philosopher and Teacher

Attention

This is the topic our workshop attendees tell us is the most challenging for them. How will you grab the audience's attention from the very start? Assuming the use of pyrotechnics would be frowned upon, what techniques can you implement in a corporate setting to captivate the audience from the start? The answer will depend mostly on the speaker's style and the audience. There are several methods you can use to get the audience's attention.

- Startling fact, statistic or statement
- Quotation
- Story
- Illustration or metaphor
- Question

Startling Fact, Statistic or Statement

Speakers can captivate the audience's attention by pointing out a remarkable fact or by making a startling statement. The caution here is to know your audience. There is an obvious audience demographic who listens to radio shock-jock DJs like Howard Stern.[4] He is known for saying startling things to his guests just to get his listening audience's attention. Obviously in a corporate setting, we are not looking for the same shock factor as Howard Stern, but we are interested in capturing the ears of our audience.

The best way to get a feel for this is to look at some examples. Remember that not all examples we provide will be appropriate for all audiences (Now, we sound like the motion picture industry rating system. We'll keep it PG, we promise!).

What you end up choosing for your presentations must be in alignment with your purpose (goal) for the presentation, your audience and also with you and your style. We have seen many attendees in our workshops attempt to emulate other speakers with their attention element, and it falls flat because it doesn't match their style. It's not aligned with who they are and it becomes obvious when they attempt the delivery. Make sure your attention piece is in alignment with your ability to deliver it.

The shock factor: "You're fired . . . those were the last two words I heard from my manager before he walked out of my office."

This statement is definitely shocking when used in a corporate setting. If the speaker is going to deliver a message on HR compliance for downsizing, this will definitely get the attention of the managers in the audience.

Now let's look at another example:

> Two hundred fifty-seven million dollars ... that sounds like a lot of money, and it is. That's the estimated value in savings, in lieu of hotel costs, that the 305 Ronald McDonald Houses around the world provide to families, so they can stay close by their hospitalized child. Your generous giving today will allow us to open our doors to thousands more families for years to come.

This opening was used by Jan Gunter, Communications Manager at the Ronald McDonald House Charities of Austin and Central Texas[5], when she was speaking to a large group of potential donors at a luncheon. As you can imagine, she had their attention from the get-go. Presenting a startling statistic to the audience can create intrigue, motivation, inspiration, stress, anxiety, fear, or curiosity.

Understand that some statistics will stir an emotion in the audience. This is a good thing, but it can also be an unstable or volatile thing. If you generate feelings that spur action, you need to create an obvious pathway for the audience to channel that emotion toward positive change. Audience members won't do anything unless they feel something. When you can get your audience to feel, they will be more likely to take action once you ask them to move forward.

Audience members won't do anything
unless they feel something.

Quotation

Quotes are commonly used by many different speakers in very different settings. Preachers quote the saints and prophets; politicians quote former politicians; and activists quote Gandhi or Mother Teresa.

Some of the executives and senior managers in our workshops immediately discount this attention-getting option because they tell us it sounds unprofessional. Well, we admit, if one of the senior directors of a Fortune 500 company starts off a presentation to a prospective customer by quoting Aristotle, it may not go over so well.

However, if a law professor were beginning his lecture on logical arguments to a group of lawyers at a convention, he might get a very different response. Aristotle wrote 60 chapters in three books on rhetoric, documenting skills on persuasion and logical influence.[6] The attorneys in attendance would respect Aristotle's insights. So without sounding overly repetitive: know your audience, know your purpose, and then decide whether a quote could work for them.

So a speaker might open with, "It's not what we do that makes us different. It's how we do it. I first heard those words from Jerry Collins when he was CEO of this company, and I was working in our service delivery department as a project manager. Twenty-three years later, I'm in the role of CEO and his words have never been truer."

It is not always necessary to quote someone that everyone in the world knows. The person you quote may only be known to the members of your audience. In the example above, the speaker is quoting a former CEO of the company where they work. The quote is relevant and it hits home with the audience because they have a personal connection to the man who spoke it.

Whether they know him personally or worked for the company when he was CEO doesn't matter because they work for the company now. That CEO, based on his history with the company, has certainly made an impact on the company today. The power of the quote is multiplied when it is combined with the power of the personal connection to the one who spoke it.

Let's try another:

Yogi Berra, the Hall of Fame catcher for the New York Yankees, once said, "If you don't know where you're going, you'll probably end up someplace else."[7] As crazy as that quote sounds, it says a lot about how we've approached product development over the past two years. Today we are dedicating ourselves to a new vision for our future. We know where we're going. We've developed our plan. We're going to move on that plan ... because we don't want to end up some place else.

Whether the individuals in the audience are New York Yankees fans, baseball fans or even sports fans doesn't matter. Knowing Yogi Berra is not necessary to understanding the profound silliness of the quote and how it applies to the future of this company. Quoting someone that is either unknown or unfamiliar to an audience can be done. One word of caution is to make certain the quote alone, regardless of who said it, supports the point you want to make in the presentation.

And another:

When I finished speaking at the XT Launch Event in Las Vegas, one woman from the audience came up to me afterwards and said, "Having a plan is only half the equation. Without the heart the hands won't follow." I thanked her, but before I could talk to her more, she was lost in the shuffle of guests as the crowd migrated out to the main exhibition floor. She's right; we won't succeed unless our hearts are in this.

In this example, the speaker is quoting a nameless, faceless individual. Even though the quoted individual does not have the credibility of being a world-famous politician, entrepreneur, or sports figure, this example still works because of the quote and the direct connection to the audience. Quotes that are profound enough to make you slow down and think can be an enlightening experience. Consider using quotations from unknown sources only if you can see a direct correlation to the audience and your message.

Keep in mind that when you use a quotation, you do not always need to provide the author. For example, some quotes are so common that everyone knows you are not trying to take credit for the creative remark. With these quotes, most will realize they have heard it before, but no one will think you are trying to claim rights to inventing the phrase. For example, the phrase "When the going gets tough, the tough get going!" is a well-known phrase that can be effective without knowing the source.[8]

Story

Everyone loves a good story, but not all the time. What we mean is that you must always consider the audience and your purpose before you decide to use a story to grab their attention. For example, if you are presenting a 20-minute summary to a group of C-Level executives on a proposed project for your department, they may not be interested in a 5-minute story about how you had to wait on a plumber at your house, even if it is directly related to your initiative for improved customer service.

Remember, there is a reason why it is called an executive summary. Think about an executive summary for a 40-page report. First, how long is it? It is probably only one page in length! Second, where is the executive summary located in the report? It is right on top! Executives want the short version of the story, and they want you to cut to the chase, providing just the facts.

Now, say you take that same group of executives on a weekend retreat to go fly-fishing. The fishing guide stands up to speak with the group the night before their fishing excursion. While he is speaking, do you think the executives would appreciate a good fishing story, especially if it were also tied to leadership? I bet they would.

Sure, it is the same audience, but the context and the content of the presentation changed. Think about your purpose for speaking and your audience before you incorporate stories. The method for developing and delivering effective stories is so important to a speaker's toolbox we have dedicated all of Chapter Seven to corporate storytelling.

Here's another example:

Before I started this project I called Joe Callahan, the former lead project manager on the Arus Aluminum account. He told me how the original deployment of services three years ago was a struggle because none of the initial application servers or networking equipment had been delivered to our datacenter in Paris, Texas, by the Friday start date. The first thought was, "Oh no, what if they were shipped to Paris, France?!?" but of course we knew that couldn't happen without international paperwork.

Joe received a call from Arus asking for the status of the project because they would have their IT auditors arriving at our datacenter in exactly one week to complete their inspections of the racked and wired infrastructure. Our timeframe for racking and wiring was getting tight. Joe pulled up the internal system we developed for provisioning and shipping equipment to our data centers. He tabbed through the form to look at the fields before he queried the shipping company for his missing shipment. He noticed something. When you type the letter T into the state field for shipping, the first state to come up in the abbreviation list is TN for Tennessee. Joe made one phone call to the shipping company and found all the equipment sitting on a loading dock in Paris, Tennessee.

After that, Joe had the developers make a change to our internal logistics database. And now the state field jumps immediately to TX instead of TN when you type the letter T for the shipping state. Joe corrected the problem at hand for Arus, but he also prevented the problem from ever occurring again.

This story could be used by a manager opening an annual awards banquet to call attention to the need for every employee to look for opportunities to improve services. The story of Joe's initiative would connect with all the attendees at the banquet.

Stories need to have a point and they need to be related to the topic at hand. If you take the audience on a ride, even if it is an enjoyable one, they may feel cheated if they cannot learn from the experience. When considering what story to tell, always start with the end in mind. Ask yourself, "What is the point I'm trying to make here?" After you have determined the point you want to make, then you need to research to find the story that fits.

There are several sources you can pull from when looking for an appropriate story. Well-known stories like the story of Colonel Sanders of KFC or Thomas Edison and inventing the light bulb after more than 10,000 failed attempts can be effective. But keep in mind that some stories are so well-known, they have lost their originality.

If you're looking for story options, a great place to look is research on historical figures. But be cautious when researching on the Internet because not every site is a reliable source for information. If you like to read, some very powerful stories can be found in historical biographies. Historical biographies have been researched to include much of the unknown background story to the well known historical references. One popular radio newsman who made use of this technique was Paul Harvey with his radio segment called *The Rest of the Story.*[9] It was the unknown story behind a person or place you knew very well, and it was always intriguing.

Of course, one of the most effective types of stories to share is a personal story. When you actually lived the story you can share so much more insight and passion with the audience. One comment we hear from workshop attendees is "I don't have any stories. I've got nothing interesting to share." That isn't true. Each one of us is living our story.

We live our life through our stories, all day, every day. It could be a family canoeing trip in Canada, an interaction with the chef at a restaurant, or even a conversation with your child on the drive to school. It takes time and effort to reflect on your stories and record them for later use. Get in the habit of keeping a journal of interesting stories and situations you encounter. You will probably be surprised how many stories you have to share.

> "Anyone can tell a story.
> Take some things that happen to you,
> dress them up, shuffle them about,
> add a dash of excitement, a little color,
> and there you have it."
> **—Lloyd Alexander,** Author

Illustrations and Metaphors

Different from a story, an illustration or a metaphor paints a picture for the audience to relate to a situation. Neuroscience tells us we are visual creatures and we remember much better with pictures than simply with words.[10] This is the reason why so many will say they are horrible at remembering names, but they are pretty good at remembering faces. To tap into that power, the speaker can use a metaphor or an illustration to paint a picture in the minds of the audience.

For example, instead of saying, "We lost over $630 million last year," you could say, "If you were to take $1 bills, lay them end to end at the equator, and circle the entire Earth twice, that would be the equivalent of how much money we lost last year—$630 million. You might be saying, 'So what? If it didn't hurt our stock price, then what's the big deal?'

"Well, what if we had recovered that money and donated it to a charity? What would that $630 million buy? It could have built 32 new soup kitchens across the country. It could have provided diapers for a year to 300,000 single moms. It could have fed over 86,000 homeless people for a year. Maybe it didn't cost us personally or in our 401k, but the opportunity cost based on what we could have done with that money is priceless . . . which means that not making a change for this year is senseless."

Most of us have never seen $630 million in cash. It is hard for us to imagine that amount of money (unless you're Donald Trump) so we cannot truly appreciate its meaning and value. To let the audience know exactly how much money that is, the speaker used an illustration to paint a picture of how much money that is. In the continuation of the illustration, the speaker made it much more personal by showing us not just the magnitude of the amount of money, but the true value of the money. She showed her audience that $630 million can buy a lot!

Louie Giglio, a pastor and speaker, does an amazing job using a golf ball metaphor to represent the Earth when he speaks about the size of the universe[11]. Canis Majoris is a star in our universe so large it could contain 7 quadrillion Earths inside of it. Wow! But just how big is a quadrillion? How many of us can actually picture a quadrillion of anything? To provide us with the proper perspective on the enormity of 7 quadrillion of anything, Giglio equates it to the entire state of Texas being covered with golf balls 22 inches deep. Now that is a lot of golf balls! And, that is a big star!

Here's another example using a metaphor:

The separation of the public facing network and the application network with a DMZ is the same concept as a high-rise office building having a security checkpoint and an elevator bank on the 40th floor where you can catch another elevator to reach the floors above that, but there is no direct path from the floors above 40 to the floors below 40. The 40th floor is the DMZ.

Drawing a diagram by creating a similarity between the real and the imagined can be done with a metaphor. This tool allows the speaker to tap into the audience's past experiences and relate them to a new and unfamiliar topic. Understanding the new concept becomes much easier once it is explained in the context of something familiar. Teachers and instructors are usually well armed with metaphors for their training and workshops. If you are delivering an informational presentation, metaphors can be a valuable tool to facilitate understanding of a complex topic for your audience.

Question

A question can be delivered at the start of a presentation to grab the audience's attention. Speakers will commonly use a rhetorical question to begin a presentation. In other words, you're asking a question without really looking for anyone to answer. You just want them to think about it.

After you ask the thought-provoking question, you must pause for about two seconds to actually provoke the thought. Understand that if you pause for longer than that, it will tend to create some tension or anxiety in the audience and someone will probably think you really want an answer. Next thing you know a person is shouting out an answer from the crowd. The flipside is that if you don't pause at all, the audience will not have a chance to actually put their mental gears in motion. Just know that a pause of at least two seconds after asking a question usually does the trick. We'll explore the power of the pause more in Chapter Eight.

Here are a few examples of rhetorical questions that might be used to kick off a speech:

"How many times a year do you think loose clothing gets caught in our manufacturing equipment?"

"What do you think is the number one fear in America?"

"As a corporate citizen, what is our responsibility to the community?"

Asking a pertinent question can engage the brains of the audience. When delivered well, the audience will be intrigued and anxious for the answer. If you ask a question that pulls the audience in, be prepared to give the answer. If you decide to hold the answer until later in the presentation, you will create tension or anxiety in their minds. It is possible their minds will check out from listening to you because now they are trying to solve the puzzle you have presented to them.

"If there are no stupid questions,
then what kind of questions do stupid people ask?
Do they get smart just in time to ask questions?"
—**Scott Adams**, Creator of the Dilbert Comic Strip and Author

Body

The third piece of the CABA opening is the Body. This is not the actual body of the presentation; it is just a preview of the body. In the past, you may have heard the expression, "Tell 'em what you're gonna tell 'em, then tell 'em, then tell 'em what you told 'em."[12] The Body section of the opening would be the "tell 'em what you're gonna tell 'em," part.

Think of it this way, the audience is not going to get on the tour bus with you if they don't even know where the bus is going. Tell them where the bus is going. Tell them where your presentation is going. You don't have to provide a tremendous amount of detail, but they do need to know the destination. Mysterious content destinations might work in some movie thrillers, but in a business presentation, the audience wants to be assured from the start they are in the right place and not wasting their time.

Have you ever taken a flight and before they shut the main cabin door they made this announcement, "Good afternoon, we will be taking off shortly for Houston. If Houston is not your destination or in your travel plans, please come forward and tell us now or it will be in your travel plans soon."

Can you imagine going to an airport where the flight attendants only told you where the plane was going after you were on board and the main cabin door was shut? If the destination is St. Lucia in the West Indies you might not mind, but when they are sending you to the West Coast and you have an important meeting in the morning on the East Coast, you will not be happy. Our point? Don't hold your audiences hostage. Tell them right from the start where you intend to take them.

Here are a few "Tell 'em what you're gonna tell 'em" examples:

"Today I will share with you the three areas of concern for this project deployment and how we plan on handling each one."

"Our discussion will focus on our sales quoting process."

"For this week's update of the department P&L numbers, I'll focus on the areas we need to address before the end of this quarter."

Audience

Ultimately, the audience wants to know from the very start of the presentation if it will be beneficial to them. They want you, the speaker, to relate to them and connect with them. When we customize our workshops for companies in different industries, we get asked questions during the breaks like, "How long did you have to research our company to understand our lingo?" We take that as a compliment because what this audience member is really saying is, "I appreciate you taking the time to get to know our company. You are speaking our language and the information is pertinent to us."

How will you relate to your audience? You need to place yourself on their team. They should see you as an expert, but also as someone compassionate about their journey. You connect with the audience by showing them that you are one of them. Join their team. Support their cause. Enable them to achieve more.

> "Don't tell people everything you know.
> Tell them what THEY need to know."
> —**Jerry Weissman**, Presentations Coach and Author

Relating to the audience can be done in several ways. One method is to use *we* statements: "Here at XLM Industries, we make safety our highest priority. We all have someone expecting us home for dinner tonight." In this example, the speaker has empathized with the audience and is clearly one of them. The speaker may have an 8 to 5 desk job and not a manufacturing position out on the shop floor, but regardless, the speaker is placing himself on the same team when it comes to making safety their highest priority.

Have you ever noticed when two people meet for the first time and begin a conversation that the first part of the conversation is spent asking questions and looking for common interests? As soon as a common interest is found, they both stay on that subject and begin sharing experiences and knowledge. As a speaker, you need to know your audience. You're looking for a way to show them you share a common interest. By completing your audience analysis you can get to know them. Now, you need to connect with them by showing the common interests you have with them, including mutual goals, needs, or concerns.

So, how else can this look in practice? Here's an example:

> As I prepared the proposal for this project, I used the information you provided and focused on the goals we want to see—timely deployment of the infrastructure, 99.999 percent uptime, and a reliable change management process. All of these are important to our organization.

This speaker is selling to a customer and has combined the preview of the body with a connection to the audience. She is making them very aware that the body of the presentation was created through the observation of the common goals they both have on this project.

CABA Will Give You a Strong First Impression

The first few seconds of your presentation should be considered prime real estate. In those first few seconds your audience is sizing up you, your presentation and the organization you represent.

Don't waste that prime opportunity by delivering an opening that sounds like every other corporate presentation they have heard. "Hi, my name is _____ and today I'm going to talk about _____." When audiences hear that standard opening, their ears turn off and their brains check out.

Remember that CABA can be delivered in any order as long as all four ingredients are included. Based on our experience, our recommendation for delivering these four elements is to start with the "A" for Attention. Because once you get their attention in those first few seconds, you've bought yourself an additional 30 seconds of audience attention. Now that you have them interested from the start, they're going to expect a rock-solid close at the end of this presentation (more details on this in Chapter Five).

Examples of opening a presentation using the CABA method:

Bill Kreiger opening a presentation using the CABA method
http://www.CorporateOvations.com/billopening

Kevin Karschnik opening a workshop using the CABA method
http:// www.CorporateOvations.com/kevinopening

—————— CHAPTER HIGHLIGHTS ——————

- When you take the stage, your audience will collect enough information in the first few seconds to create a first impression of you and your presentation. Regardless of how quickly it occurs or how long the impression lasts, understand that you will be evaluated from the very start of your presentation.

- The formula we use for opening a presentation includes four key elements: Credibility, Attention, Body, and Audience (or CABA for short). When all four pieces are delivered to the audience, you will capture the listeners from the very beginning. These four pieces can be delivered to the audience in any order.

  › Credibility—The audience wants to know your background on this topic.

  › Attention—The technique implemented to captivate the audience from the start. There are several methods you can use:

    - Startling fact, statistic or statement
    - Quotation
    - Story
    - Illustration or metaphor
    - Question

  › Body—This is a preview of the body of your presentation.

  › Audience—From the very start of the presentation, let the audience know how the presentation will be beneficial to them.

——————— TOMORROW'S CHALLENGE ———————

As you prepare for your next presentation, answer these questions:

- ☐ What perception or impression do I want my audience to have as I begin to speak?

- ☐ What can I do or say from the very start to capture my audience's attention?

- ☐ How can I implement CABA for my next presentation?

CHAPTER 5

Close with Confidence

*"Make sure you have finished speaking
before your audience has finished listening."*

—Dorothy Sarnoff, Actress and Speech Coach

James is an accounting manager for a Tulsa manufacturing plant. He just discussed the quarterly numbers with the plant manager and several executives from the corporate office. After making his final statement about missing the targets this quarter by 4 percent, he pauses and stares out at the audience. Then, he says, "Well, that's all I have for you today. We need to keep working on bringing those numbers up for next quarter. Thanks."

As he powers down his laptop and collects his scattered paperwork, a hand goes up from the audience. James immediately realizes he didn't take any questions. "Oh, I'm sorry," he says, "Are there any questions?"

Have you ever been in a presentation like this? The content throughout may have been informative and well structured, but the end just turns into a train wreck. There was no summary of the key elements, there was no action item or call for change, and there was absolutely nothing memorable about it at all.

When developing a presentation, always begin with your end in mind.[1] If you want to receive a corporate ovation, you need to carefully construct and deliver an effective and impactful presentation close.

> "All that matters is the ending;
> it's the most important part. . . ."
> —**Johnny Depp**, Actor and Film Producer

The Close Is Vitally Important

Have you ever seen a disappointing movie? You know the type. You are watching, engaged throughout, somewhat intrigued by the mystery of it all. You look down at your watch in the movie theater and notice that you are almost two full hours into the movie, and the end cannot be far away. You start asking yourself, "How is this going to end? I don't see how this is going to get resolved in only a few short minutes? I'm not sure what the outcome is going to be."

Then the movie finally ends with all the characters walking out of the scene. There's no real closure or relief from the tension that had been building throughout the movie. You're left thinking, *That's it?*

Or how often has a friend been telling you about a movie and he ends by saying, "but I didn't really like the ending"? Rarely do you hear someone say, "It was okay, but I didn't really care for the opening." How the movie finishes can make or break the movie. Sometimes the Blu-Ray or DVD versions of movies will feature an alternate ending in their bonus materials. Often those alternate endings leave you with unresolved issues or tension from the storyline. That's why the director selected the ending that brought closure to the story.

When there is anything left unresolved, it is most likely the setup for a sequel. In the movie *Batman Begins*[2], the final scene has Batman on a rooftop speaking to Commissioner Gordon. The ending provides closure to the story as they discuss the Scarecrow getting captured, but they set up a sequel when Gordon reveals there are others who escaped from Arkham Asylum who are still at large. Gordon specifically creates audience excitement and anticipation for the sequel when he hands Batman a piece of evidence and says, "He leaves this as his calling card."

Batman turns the card over to see it's a Joker. The final two lines of dialogue in the movie remind the audience of Batman's mission to deliver justice without seeking personal glory. Batman stands for justice in the corrupt world of Gotham while everyone else seeks power and money at any cost. Gordon says, "I never said thank you." Batman, perched on the ledge of the building turns back to Gordon and says, "And you'll never have to." Then, with the sound of his cape in the wind, Batman leaps off the building and glides down into the crime filled streets of Gotham. The end.

Batman Begins movie ending
http://www.CorporateOvations.com/batmanending

While the quarterly review of a company's financial numbers is not necessarily Hollywood material, there is something we can learn by analyzing the ending to movies, plays, symphonies, and professional presentations. Each of these can create curiosity and tension throughout the delivery. By the end, the audience wants all of that tension resolved and all questions answered. When done effectively, the end of the performance wraps everything up and the audience rises to their feet with applause, wanting more.

In a symphony, the music will build to a crescendo and then taper down to an ending with closure. Movies and plays will tie up loose ends and provide a reminder of the key point from the story. As we've seen from *Batman Begins*, Batman summarizes his moral character with his final line, Gordon sets up the sequel revealing the Arkham Asylum escapees, and the Joker card creates a memorable event for the audience. In a similar fashion, professional speakers will provide a summary of the key elements given to the audience, along with instructions on what to do next. Finally, the speaker will leave the audience with something memorable to reinforce the key message in the audience's long-term memory.

Whether you are speaking to your team at the office, representing your company on the stage at a trade show, or delivering a message to the local Rotary Club[3], your audience deserves no less. They deserve a prepared conclusion to help them make the most of the information shared with them.

The MAS Formula

The formula used by professional speakers includes three key elements—Memorable, Action, and Summary. We call it MAS. If you are fluent in Spanish, you know this means "more." And that's a great way to remember it. In other words, your goal should be that you always leave your audiences wanting more.

> "The secret of a good sermon is to have
> a good beginning and a good ending,
> then having the two as close together as possible."
> **—George F. Burns,** Comedian, Actor, and Writer

Too often, speakers overlook the close to a presentation. At best, they realize they should include a call to action for the audience.

While a call to action is great, it is just one of the three elements that make up a truly effective and impactful closing.

When you include all three parts of MAS in your close, your audience will appreciate the information you provided and will be motivated to improve based on the information they've received from you. These three pieces, much like the CABA formula for opening a presentation, can be delivered in any sequence. You just need to make sure all three of them are included.

The three ingredients of MAS
(Memorable, Action, and Summary)
can be delivered to the audience in any order.

Memorable

In the news industry, it is called a sound bite. When a reporter wants to pull a piece of a speech, they are always looking for the one line that sums up the entire message. It is the one part of the message that aligns with the theme and is also memorable in its delivery. One great example would be Ronald Reagan's speech at the Berlin Wall in June of 1987.

Can you recall the most memorable sound bite from that speech? If you guessed, "Mr. Gorbachev, tear down this wall,"[4] you're right! This one line pretty much sums up the entire theme of his speech and the action to be taken. While you may not be the President of the United States speaking to the world, making your presentation memorable will help your audience remember what you said and will help them understand what they should do with what you gave them.

Ronald Reagan's famous speech at the Berlin Wall
http://www.CorporateOvations.com/reaganberlin

For crafting the *memorable* portion of your close, you can use any of the attention tools defined in the previous chapter on opening your presentation with power (e.g. a startling fact or statistic, quotation, story, illustration or metaphor, or a question).

Here's an example of a speaker using a quotation to drive home the fact that fiscal responsibility is not only necessary, but also critical. He needs his audience to start questioning and reviewing every expense if they plan on correcting the problem at hand:

> It's been said that a penny saved is a penny earned. If we are going to get our department back into fiscal shape, no cost is too immaterial to review.

In some cases, you may choose to provide the audience with bookends for your presentation. A bookend close is when you complete a thought or story you started in the opening of your presentation.

As we touched on in the last chapter, in his radio segment, *The Rest of the Story*, Paul Harvey was a great storyteller. His ability to bookend was one of the things that made the segment so great. While the stories he told were always intriguing, the best part always came at the end when he would reveal to you the full name of the main character in the story.

It would be someone everyone knew, but we had never known about that part of his or her life. He would always close this segment with the same line, " ... and now you know ... the rest of the story! I'm Paul Harvey ... Good day![5]" A bookend in the memorable portion of your close is when you give the audience *the rest of the story*.

Tom Gorey, National Director of Business Partner Programs for XO Communications[6], used this technique to close his presentation to his new sales team. He said, "At the beginning of my presentation I told you about my childhood home and the trees outside my bedroom window. I always wondered how high those trees would reach. There was no limit to how high they would go. Well, I live in Seattle now, but my bed is still right next to the window. Each night I go to bed wondering how high those trees will reach. And each day I come to work thinking about the opportunity we have here and I wonder how high our team will reach."

A safety manager for a manufacturing plant ended his speech by saying, "Safety in our company is always the highest priority. As you heard at the start of my presentation, that young repair technician took a short cut with a repair in our plant. As a result, a young man lost his hand. As the safety manager for this plant, I can assure you, I will never allow shortcuts in repairs just to get the line moving again . . . because I was that young repair technician. Now I have to live with that for the rest of my life. Safety is our highest priority."

You may be reading these examples and thinking, "Wow! That all sounds a little too dramatic for my weekly project updates to the team." We are not looking for drama here. Anything you deliver needs to feel right to you. All we ask is that you stretch your creativity beyond what you may have done in the past.

Randy Pausch created a memorable close in his "Last Lecture" at Carnegie Mellon with these words, "It's not about how to achieve your dreams. It's about how to lead your life. If you lead your life the right way, the karma will take care of itself. The dreams will come to you."[7]

Or, how about this example:

This error on our part only cost us a few hours of service to the customer. And thankfully, the customer relationship was not terminally damaged. If we don't invest in our infrastructure for the delivery of our services then we need to ask ourselves a question, "What will be the cost of our next error?" It could be much more than just a few hours of interrupted service . . . it could be the entire customer relationship.

Or, this one:

In short, we are behind on our provisioning schedule because the workload is more than we initially expected. We will transfer the application network to Tasha, one of our senior project managers. The transfer will not be considered complete until I receive the acknowledgment from Tasha that she has uploaded all of the project requirements to her workspace. Much like the transfer of piloting a naval vessel from one helmsman to another is not completed until the relieving helmsman states, 'helm has been relieved,' I'll confirm the transfer with your team as soon as Tasha confirms.

Action

In Chapter 2, you learned the importance of knowing the purpose of a presentation when you are preparing. As you may recall, you have to ask yourself, *What is my goal? What am I trying to achieve? What is the ideal outcome for this presentation?* The answer to all of these questions will reveal the purpose of your presentation.

The Action component of your close will align with the purpose of your presentation and provide a foundation for persuading your audience.[8] In a sense, it tests for the success of your presentation. The action of the close will be the answer to your purpose.

For example, if your purpose is to gain approval on your budget from the senior leadership team, then in the action segment of your close, you will ask the senior leaders to approve the budget. If your purpose is to educate the sales team on the new interface for placing orders, then in the action segment you will confirm the audience's understanding of what to do with the new skills and techniques learned. If your purpose is to inform the senior leadership on the status of a project, then the action segment of your close will confirm their understanding of the current status.

If there is an action to be taken as a result of your presentation, this is where you tell the audience what they need to do with their new knowledge. The action can be presented in various forms including a question, a challenge, an invitation, or a statement. The method you choose for framing your action in the close will depend on your style, your audience, and your purpose.

Question

The question in the action segment can come across as fairly direct to the audience. If you choose to use a question to motivate your audience to action, be careful with your word choice, vocal inflections and body language as you deliver it. You will get more advice on delivery techniques in Chapters 8 and 9.

Here are a few examples of questions that might be used in the action segment of a close:

> "Based on our analysis and projections, we will need to increase our budget by 10 percent next year. I'd like to ask you now if you will approve this increase for next year."

> "We cannot just sit on our hands while our community holds its hand out. What can you do today to make a difference in our community?"

> "With the projected returns we see for this financial model, who would want to vote 'no' on this project? Can I get everyone's approval to start today?"

Challenge

You hear challenges issued by professional speakers, motivational speakers and classroom teachers all the time. Challenges are issued to create a certain level of anxiety within the audience. The stress created is usually just enough to motivate the audience to move. After all, everyone loves the feeling of overcoming a challenge!

However, caution should be taken because, if delivered improperly, a challenge can be interpreted by the audience as a juvenile "double-dog-dare" coming from the speaker. We all know from the movie *A Christmas Story*[9] how effective the double-dog-dare is with young boys, but with a group of senior managers at your company, maybe not so much.

As with using a question to prompt action, *how* you present the challenge visually, verbally and vocally can determine whether or not your audience is receptive to the challenge or offended by it. If you are not sure how it will be received, practice the delivery of your challenge with a peer and get their honest feedback.

Here are a couple of examples:

> "I challenge you to take what you've learned here today and implement just one new technique. If you do that, you're going to find a natural progression in your sales conversations leading you closer to that trusted advisor relationship."

> "So, we all walk away with a new challenge for our departments. Decrease your travel expenditures by 8 percent for the last quarter, and you will put us all in a better position for our profitability bonus at year end."

Invitation

When you are seeking the same type of action as the challenge, but the challenge sounds a bit too harsh or direct, you can soften it by changing it to an invitation. Who doesn't like to get an invitation to something? Even if you can't attend or don't want to attend, isn't it nice to know you were invited? You can play on that truth about human nature by inviting your audience to participate in a program or implement new skills.

Here are a couple of examples:

> "I invite you to try one of the new sales techniques we discussed today. What you will find is that you will start to build your own brand as a salesperson. When you build your

personal brand, customers will call you. When you build your personal brand, customers will be loyal."[10]

"Community service is not someone else's responsibility. It's ours. The opportunity to participate in a Habitat for Humanity[11] build is an open invitation to make a difference in the lives of others. It's an open invitation personalized with your name on it. You're invited. I hope you will RSVP with a yes. I know I will."

Statement

While it is the speaker's purpose to achieve a goal, the speaker cannot make the audience take action. Ultimately, it is up to the audience to decide if they want to act on what they have learned. Even if the audience decides they will act, they will also need to decide how to implement what they have learned. If you use a statement for the action element of your close, you simply lay it all at the feet of the audience. The rest is up to them. The audience must decide if and how they will use the information.

Here are a few examples:

"Based on the project status, which is currently ahead of schedule by two days, I need to thank each of you for the support of your departments. As issues arise, I am confident that we will work through those situations in the same manner."

"The changes to the email routable addresses will propagate across the mail servers of the internet over night. I request your understanding in this process as email may be spotty over the next 48 hours."

"The new CRM upgrade is targeted to improve our call center response times by 43 seconds on average. While a few seconds doesn't sound like much, it means thousands of dollars to our bottom line. The success of this upgrade can serve as a template for future projects that may affect all of your departments."

Summary

Before wrapping up your presentation, you need to tell the audience where they have been. In the opening of the presentation we told them where the bus was going. Now that the tour is over, give them a quick recap on where the bus went.

When you recap the presentation, it should not include a lot of detail. It should be kept short or else the audience will become annoyed, as it seems like you are telling them all the same information a second time.

Providing too lengthy of a summary in your close can be bad for you in two ways. First, your audience may think you have forgotten what you already told them. Second, they may think you don't think very highly of them because you are repeating yourself, as if they need another lesson before they could possibly understand. That will be seen as condescending. So keep your summary short and simple, even as short as one sentence.

Here are some examples:

"Today we discussed the three critical success factors for my department next year."

"I've shared with you the method for opening a trouble ticket, how to escalate a ticket and finally how to properly close a ticket."

"These are the updated numbers for the quarter and our current focus points."

"So today's talk was about my childhood dreams, enabling the dreams of others, and some lessons learned."[12]

Just like the CABA formula for opening, the MAS formula does not have to be delivered in a given order to be effective. The three ingredients can be rearranged in whatever format is most comfortable and natural for you. In many cases, the summary makes a great transition from the body of the presentation to the close. The summary serves as the signal to the audience that "We're all done! No more new information! I'm going to wrap things up right now."

Always Leave Them Wanting More

Most audiences are more alert during the close of a presentation because they recognize that it is coming to an end.[13] This is your opportunity to leave the audience with a lasting impression.

Our formula is not intended to be overly dramatic; it is intended to be effective. And the best method for being effective is to gain the attention of your audience.

One way to do that is by differentiating yourself from every other business presentation they've seen. Your audience deserves more in your presentation closing than just, "Well, that's all folks." Give them something memorable so they don't forget your message. Call them to action with specific instructions on what to do next. Give them a summary of the key points or the theme for the day. It is a simple formula that goes a long way. Once you have the CABA for the opening and the MAS for the close, you are ready to construct the body of your presentation.

Examples of closing a presentation using the MAS method:

Cynthia Oelkers closing a Facilitation Skills Workshop
http://www.CorporateOvations.com/cynthiaclose

Russ Peterson Jr. closing a Leading Teams Workshop
http://www.CorporateOvations.com/russclose

—————— **CHAPTER HIGHLIGHTS** ——————

- How you close a presentation is critical because the last thing an audience hears just might be the one thing they remember. Your audience deserves more in your presentation closing than just, "Well, that's all folks."

- The formula we use for closing a presentation includes three key elements: Memorable, Action, and Summary (or MAS for short). These three pieces can be delivered to the audience in any order.

  › *Memorable*—The technique implemented to help your main message stick. There are several methods you can use:
    - Startling fact, statistic or statement
    - Quotation
    - Story
    - Illustration or metaphor
    - Question

  › *Action*—The component used to challenge or invite your audience to do something with the information you provided. It should align with the purpose for your presentation and tell the audience what they need to do with their new knowledge.

  › *Summary*—This is a review of the body of your presentation.

—————— TOMORROW'S CHALLENGE ——————

As you prepare for your next presentation, answer these questions:

☐ What final impression do I want to leave with my audience?

☐ What can I do or say at the end of my presentation to help make my message stick?

☐ How will I challenge or invite my audience to take action on the information I provided?

CHAPTER 6

Structure the Presentation Body

"A theme is a memory aid; it helps you through the presentation just as it also provides the thread of continuity for your audience."

—Dave Carey, Motivational Speaker, Consultant and Author

The year is 350 B.C. and Aristotle has just called his class to order. Thius, one of his students, walks to the center of the forum and begins speaking by addressing his teacher first.

"In my oration today, I offer my theory on causes for the changing shapes of the moon." Before Thius is allowed to continue, Aristotle rises from his seat and the room becomes silent as the students wait for the great teacher to speak. He says, "If you are to provide any theory in this forum for our consideration, you must provide three forms of proof to substantiate your theory and observations."

After a long moment of awkward silence, Thius turns back toward the audience and walks quietly back to his seat. So maybe it didn't happen exactly like that, but Aristotle[1] knew what it took to be persuasive. How do we know this? Because he recorded his thoughts in his *Rhetoric,* three books and 60 chapters on how to be a persuasive and influential speaker.

Documented in his *Rhetoric,* Aristotle pointed out the need to appeal to an audience with a minimum of three forms of proof. He also documented his three methods for doing just that through ethos (credibility), pathos (emotions) and logos (logic). Now, almost 2,400 years later, his *Rhetoric* is still applicable today. All 60 chapters of his *Rhetoric* can be summarized into three key elements that are required for an effective presentation body:

- The body of the presentation must be delivered properly.
- It must be structured.
- It must contain an appeal to the audience.

The Body of the Presentation Must Be Delivered Properly

Proper delivery of your presentation is the focus in Chapters 8 and 9, where we will share techniques on how to deliver your message visually, verbally and vocally for the greatest impact on the audience. For now, we will focus on the structure of the body and how to appeal to the audience.

The Body of the Presentation Must Be Well Structured

Without structure to the body of a presentation, your audience is going to be lost. In most cases, when an audience member is lost, they will immediately look for something to reconnect them to the message. If they do not find something in your message to reconnect quickly, they will check out of the presentation and proceed to connect elsewhere, usually with their smart phone.

Even with structure to the body in place, if the speaker does a poor job of transitioning from one body point to the next, the audience may realize at some point that they have already missed something. When you are the speaker, think of yourself as a tour guide on a bus with a group of eager tourists anxious to take in the sites. In the opening of your presentation, you provided a preview of the body of the message. Like a tour guide, you told the individuals, "This tour bus will be visiting the ancient ruins, the downtown aquarium, and the tallest building in the world!" Based on the preview in your presentation opening, the audience thought, "This sounds great! I'm jumping on the bus!"

Now that the bus has started the tour and the speaker is into the body of the presentation, the attendees want to have these amazing attractions pointed out to them. Nobody would want to miss these exciting sights!

Now, let's assume that someone on the tour bus raises their hand and says, "I thought we were going to see the ancient ruins. Where are they?" The tour guide responds, "Oh, we already passed the ruins about five minutes ago. You missed them." How frustrated do you think that person would be? She invested all this time on a bus tour to see three amazing sights and now the first attraction is history . . . and she missed it! Audience members feel cheated when they have invested time in attending a presentation only to find that the speaker's presentation is difficult to follow.

Or think about it this way: Have you ever been lost? We mean *really* lost. As a child, did you ever get lost in a department store? Or as an adult, while driving in a different city? It's not fun. In the same way that these experiences call up strong feelings of anxiety and tension, audience members who cannot follow a speaker through a presentation may also experience anxiety and tension.

Presentations that are not structured and concise can make audience members feel trapped. In fact, you may be experiencing some tension right now as these words bring back the memory of a bad presentation you saw.

The biggest mistake we see from presenters is the speaker's perceived need to overpopulate the body of the presentation. The assumption seems to be that if you provide a little bit of everything, there will be something for everyone. We call this the *show up and throw up* method of presenting. This mistaken logic tells them that if they provide all the information they have, no one will be able to say, "You didn't cover what I wanted." This notion is ill conceived and incorrect. A well-structured presentation will be much more effective, making it memorable and thought-provoking.[2]

The 9-Minute Presentation™

People tend to provide too much information when presenting because a presentation with too much information is actually easier to construct. George Bernard Shaw once said, "Sorry for the letter, I didn't have time to write a postcard." He knew it would take him more time to be concise. When you don't have to think about the structure or what content you will keep or cut, you will *create* a presentation faster but your *delivery* will be longer than necessary.

From our experience with thousands of attendees at our workshops, we have found that nine minutes is an ideal length for delivering a presentation targeting a basic understanding for the audience. Now, putting together a 9-minute presentation can take longer than when you just throw in as much information as possible. But consider this: While it may take you longer to prepare a concise message, your audience will appreciate it more because you get to the point and save them time.

We have a question for you, how many people attend your presentations? If you are speaking to an audience of six at a team meeting, you will save your co-workers and the company hours! Companies and individuals have adopted the 9-minute presentation style to put an end to costly and boring presentations.

There is another reason why we recommend only nine minutes. While audience lapse of attention can be as frequent as every two minutes in lengthy presentations, research shows that you will only need to deal with one serious lapse of audience attention about halfway through a 9-minute presentation.[3] You can address that lapse with a well-constructed presentation body that incorporates engaging interactions at the mid-point. Without a well-designed structure, your audience won't be able to follow you and they'll start dropping off left and right.

Yes, quality takes time; however, we have two common structures to help expedite your process. These structures are called the *rule of three* and the *problem–solution*.

"No one can remember more than three points."
—**Philip Crosby,** Businessman and Author

The "Rule of Three" Structure

As Aristotle taught us in his *Rhetoric*, three forms of proof are substantial for a persuasive argument. Delivery of thoughts in "threes" is common and it works.[4] There must be a reason why there were three bears in the house that Goldilocks found. Or Three Little Pigs. Or Three Blind Mice.

Or how about this? Why are there usually three sizes of drinks at the fast food restaurant? Why is it three strikes and you're out? Why do we have three branches of government in the United States? Why is the triangle the strongest geometric shape in engineering? Why were there Three Stooges? Three Musketeers? Three Amigos? Why does "morning, noon, and night" sound better than "morning and night?" It's the power of three!

Sometimes it just sounds better to present things in threes. One may not be enough. Four is too many to remember. Two always seems to beg the third. Three just seems to work! In Winston Churchill's famous speech he said, "I have nothing to offer but blood, toil, tears and sweat." However, the way it is commonly remembered (because of the rule of three) is, "I have nothing to offer but blood, sweat and tears."[5]

If you have no other logical method of structuring the content of your presentation, try to fit it into three buckets, because it works. The audience will appreciate the logical presentation and they will find it easier to follow and recall your content.

> "Your purpose is to make your audience see what you saw, hear what you heard, feel what you felt. Relevant detail, couched in concrete, colorful language, is the best way to re-create the incident as it happened and to picture it for the audience."
>
> —**Dale Carnegie**, Speaker, Teacher, and Author of *The Quick and Easy Way to Effective Speaking*

In reality, it's perfectly fine to have more than three key points, or even less than three points. Just remember that a logical flow or structure is still desired by the audience. If the multiple points are random and disjointed, the audience will find it difficult to follow your message and even more difficult to remember much of the presentation. No one item will appear more significant than the other and the gravity of your argument may lose momentum.

What if your spouse provides you with a list of seemingly random items to pick up from the store? Then, on your way to the store, you realize you left the list on the counter at home. You pull out your mobile phone to call home. When your spouse answers the phone and finds the list, he or she says, "You don't need me to email this list to you. We're making ham and cheese omelets, and strawberry pancakes, your favorite!"

Now, whether it is your favorite or not, you probably know what you need now because you can picture what you are making. You can actually see the ingredients and the end result. You have placed all the ingredients into two buckets, omelets and pancakes. That is something structured and something you can easily remember, even when the list to make both of these dishes might be 15 items long.

The Problem-Solution Structure

Do you remember *The Wizard of Oz*?[6] Dorothy has landed in a strange place and she just wants to go home. This is her problem to which she sees no immediate solution. As she searches for a solution to her problem, she meets other characters along the way. Each of these characters also has a problem and they are all seeking solutions. They are told that a solution to each of their problems can be found with the Wizard of Oz. The movie unfolds into an adventure as she and her band of misfits journey to meet the Wizard.

Remember how it ends? The Lion finds his courage, the Tin Man gets a heart, the Scarecrow receives a brain, and Dorothy finds her way home to Kansas. People have said that everyone loves a happy ending. We love to hear about an adventure with struggles (the problem) where the resolution (or solution) is found in the end.

This structure is also great for corporate presentations. For example, the problem-solution structure is ideal for presenting a budgetary issue of projected cost overruns. While this type of financial presentation is not nearly as adventurous as *The Wizard of Oz*, we would all like to know the potential solutions to the budgetary issues lurking in our fiscal numbers. Using this method you can establish the problem and the importance of addressing the problem. Then, the rest of your presentation will be the journey to the solution.

The Common Theme Structure

Think about a funny comedian you have seen or heard before. Which comedic bits or routines are the easiest to recall? Most likely, the humorous moments are all tied together with a commonality. For example, Bill Cosby shares many humorous moments audience members can recall because he links them all together with a story about growing up in his house or raising five children of his own.[7]

Politicians deliver campaign trail speeches with a common theme. If the audience is not going to remember every single point they make, they will definitely remember the theme. In the 2008 U.S. Presidential elections, Barack Obama's consistent theme was "Change."[8] Whether audience members remembered every point he made or not, they could easily recall the theme from his message. Great speakers will often use themes in their messages. This makes the message much more memorable. "I have a dream!"[9]; "Ask not what your country can do for you . . ."[10]; "Tear down this wall."[11]; and "Blessed are the meek . . ."[12] are all famous examples.

The Body of the Presentation Must Appeal to the Audience

There are two key considerations when constructing a presentation built for maximum appeal with your audience. The first consideration is which type of presentation you are delivering. The type you choose depends on your defined purpose for presenting. The second consideration for audience appeal is how transitions are used to create a logical flow.

Audience Appeal depends on the Presentation Type

As we discussed in Chapter Two, presentations fall into three general categories: informative, persuasive, and entertaining. Each type of presentation will use a different technique for appealing to the audience.

The appeals are based on the purpose or objective of the presentation. Each of the three types will have different ingredients in the structure of the content to achieve its purpose. In all cases, you need to make your content sticky, which means memorable or understandable.[13]

To understand how we could structure the body content to have maximum impact with our audience, let's look at each type in more detail:

Informative Presentations

If the sole purpose of your presentation is to educate and inform, without an appeal for action, then your presentation is informative. Informative presentations will be structured according to the topic being taught.

For example, if you are teaching the group how to open a customer service ticket in the new CRM (Customer Relationship Management) System, you could structure the delivery around the key tasks each customer service representative will need to complete: How to open a ticket, how to check the status of a ticket, how to update a ticket, and finally, how to close a ticket.

For the quarterly review of your financial statements, the presentation could be structured to review the Income Statement, the Balance Sheet, and finally the Cash Flow Statement. Or if you are educating a group on how to install firewall software in a data center, you could structure the delivery around key elements such as data gathering preparation, installation of the software, and rule set installation.

Informative presentations must follow a logical flow while addressing all of the pertinent information required for complete understanding. You want the attendees to have questions on the content of the presentation, not on the structure! The more logical the delivery and flow, the more the students will internalize and comprehend.

John C. Maxwell demonstrates a structured informative presentation
http://www.CorporateOvations.com/maxwellstructure

Nearly 42 percent of all statistics are made up.

Persuasive Presentations

When you think about persuasive presentations, the first type that usually comes to mind is a sales presentation. While that is an excellent example, many other individuals outside of the sales profession deliver persuasive presentations on a regular basis. Examples include a director persuading her VP to approve her budget for the year, a manager persuading his team to buy into the new direction of the company, or maybe a project manager persuading the business unit to delay the project by another week to make sure they get the deployment right the first time.

While the body of the persuasive presentation must be easy to follow, it must also provide supporting evidence for each of the claims the person is making. In the sales example, if we attempt to persuade you to purchase your learning and development training services from iSpeak[14], we would need to present several reasons why that would be a wise decision.

The three reasons may include iSpeak provides the highest quality instructors; iSpeak provides customized curriculum; and iSpeak delivers the best customer service in the industry. As soon as we make those three statements, what is the first thing to pop into your head? "Hmmm, best instructors ... best curriculum ... best service ... that's what the last sales guy said!" If you are going to persuade the audience by providing several reasons, you must provide supporting evidence or proof for each of the claims you are making.

If a defense attorney is pleading a case in front of a jury and she says, "My client cannot be guilty because he was nowhere near the scene at the time of the crime." Of course, we'd all like to believe she is not lying to us in a court of law, but what do you think the judge and jury are thinking? "Prove it!" If the attorney can produce a ticket stub from a play the defendant was attending at the time, cell phone records that show he was placing calls from the theater at that time, and several eyewitnesses that saw him at the play, you now have proof. As a result, the judge and jury are persuaded to believe the original claim that the client was not at the crime scene.

> "Example is not the main thing
> in influencing others'
> it's the only thing."
>
> **—Albert Schweitzer,** German Theologian and Philosopher

In business, if you are going to make a claim to persuade, then you need to follow up each claim with supporting evidence as to why the audience should believe each claim. For example, we can follow up the quality instructors claim by explaining that iSpeak has a rigorous and documented process for certifying all instructors as iSpeak Certified Master Instructors (iCMI). And we can say that our instructors have been honored with awards like "Best Sales Trainer of the Year" by the American Business Awards.[15] You now have documented proof of why you should believe the initial claim that the instructors are high quality.

Some other forms of supporting materials include stories, facts, statistics, quotes from customers, case studies, examples, research, metaphors, or testimonies. Persuasion begins by presenting your reasons in a logical fashion and supporting each point with information that can be viewed as evidence to support the claim. This will help you build authentic relationships with your audience, highlight the genuine strengths of your message, and ultimately create outcomes that are in everyone's best interests.[16]

The body of the persuasive presentation
must be easy to follow and provide
supporting evidence for each claim.

Entertaining Presentations

When you have been asked to entertain your audience with a presentation, the body structure tends to become much more fluid. A common structure for an entertaining presentation is a theme. As an example, comedians who perform standup routines and provide random thoughts, stories and jokes can make audiences laugh, but afterwards, many of the jokes are hard to recall because each joke stood on its own. The jokes may have been presented in a random order.

If, on the other hand, a comedian delivers their material with a common theme, both the content and the presenter are more memorable. For example, Jeff Foxworthy has many types of jokes and stories but he is most famous for his themed jokes on "You might be a redneck if . . . "[17]

Of course, the structure of an entertaining presentation does not apply only to comedic presentations. Some entertaining presentations are captivating because the speaker is sharing an amazing story of struggle, survival and accomplishment. In these types of entertaining presentations, the flow of the delivery is best received when it follows an emotional flow structure. If you could graph the flow of this type of delivery it might resemble the letter "W."

The presentation starts off with something captivating and exciting. Then, the speaker takes the audience down into the abyss of a struggle. At some point in the middle, the speaker takes the audience to a happier or funny place. Then a slight dip again, maybe not quite as low as the first abyss, and finally, the speaker ends with a crescendo of success. Think about any speaker you have heard deliver their life's stories.

Our guess is that the speaker did not say, "Well, my life has been very good. I've never had any hardships. I was always successful. I never had to dig down deep to pull myself out of a pit. I've always had a pretty good life."

A speaker wouldn't structure the speech like that because audiences are not attracted to stories like that. They want to hear about an amazing story of struggle, a perseverance to overcome, and finally a victory! There is something programmed deep within each and every one of us that draws us to this type of story. If you are providing an entertaining message, give the audience what they want!

> "Your audience gives you everything you need.
> They tell you. There is no director
> who can direct you like an audience."
>
> —**Fanny Brice**, Comedian and Actress

Appeal to the Audience with Structured Transitions Between Your Key Points

Regardless of the structure you select, the audience needs signs or markers that tell them when you are moving on to the next key point. These are called transitions, and they serve as the road signs for your audience as they travel along this journey with you. If you are a parent, have you ever heard any of these questions from the back seat? "Are we there yet?" "Where are we?" "How much longer 'til we get there?" Your kids ask these questions because they want to know where they are in the course of their trip!

At the beginning of this chapter, we asked you if you had ever been lost. Well, when you're lost while driving, what do you look for? Signs! You look for road signs to give you a clue where you are and where you are going. And how did you get lost in the first place? You probably got distracted for a few moments and missed a turn or an exit. It happens.

Well, guess what? Your audience is no different. They are going to be distracted for a few moments[18] when their neighbor is nudging them, when their stomachs start growling, or when they receive a text message. Once they are back and they look up, will they be lost in your content? How easy will it be for them to get back on track with your message? Give them road signs to make it easier for them. Use transitions in your delivery and your audience will know where you are in the presentation.

The simplest form of transition is a simple numbering of the items you are going to discuss—first, second, third, etc. Remember our earlier example of the tour guide? As a speaker, your audience expects you to organize the sights they will see in a logical format. Then, the audience expects you to point out these amazing sights as you pass them. As we stated earlier, if the tour guide does not point out the sights as you pass them, the audience will feel cheated and that is the mark of a poor tour guide!

Now, contrast that scenario with a different tour guide. This tour guide starts by saying, "First, you are about to see the ancient ruins." With information and stories about the first sight, she creates intrigue, suspense and appreciation. This provides a kind of "mental preview" of what they are about to see. Then with a sweep of her arm she gestures out the windows on the right-hand side of the bus and the audience beholds the ruins. After the bus slows and drives past, the tour guide says, "Next, we will be moving on to the downtown aquarium." Transitions like "First," "Next," and "Finally" provide mental road signs signaling to the audience movement from one topic to the next.

> Just like a road sign, for transitions to be effective they must be easy to see.

Other methods for transition and progression through a presentation can take the form of questions, numbered steps, logical compartments of information, chronological events, or spatial locations. Regardless of the type of transition, there are two keys to creating effective transitions. First, they must work well with the structure of the content. If the presentation being delivered was a review of the order submission process for our sales team, then a description of each step with a numbered transition would be completely logical. Questions positioned as transitions may not be as effective. If the presentation was to propose changes to the current order submission process, then questions as transitions may make perfect sense.

Transitional questions may sound something like this:

> *"So, what is the most important element of the sales process?"*
> *"How do we improve in this area?"*
> *"What needs to change?"*
> *"Why is this important?"*
> *"What can we do next?"*

The second key to effective transitions is that they must be easy to see. Think of a road sign when you are driving. If a sign is not large enough, not well lit, or is placed poorly, there is a good chance you will not see the sign as you drive past it.

How do you make certain that your transitions are seen as you deliver your presentation? The answer is in *how* you deliver it. In Chapters 8 and 9, we will provide more information on *how* to deliver a presentation for the greatest results using effective words, vocal talents and our body language.

———————— **CHAPTER HIGHLIGHTS** ————————

- In 350 B.C. Aristotle documented the need to appeal to an audience in three ways through ethos (credibility), pathos (emotions) and logos (logic).

- Without structure to the body of a presentation, your audience is going to be lost and will begin to search for something to reconnect to the message (or they will start to connect to friends on their smart phone).

- Delivery of thoughts in "threes" is common and it works because audiences appreciate a logical presentation and will be able to recall your content.

- How you appeal to your audience will depend on the type of presentation you are delivering:
  - › Informative—must follow a logical flow while addressing all of the pertinent information required for complete understanding.
  - › Persuasive—must be easy to follow and provide supporting evidence for each of the claims.
  - › Entertaining—tends to become much more fluid with a theme as the common structure.

- Transitions are used as signs or markers to tell the audience when you are moving on to the next key point. These can take the form of numbered steps, questions, logical compartments of information, chronological events, or spatial locations.

―――――――― **TOMORROW'S CHALLENGE** ――――――――

As you prepare for your next presentation, answer these questions:

☐ How will you appeal to your audience through ethos (credibility), pathos (emotions) and logos (logic)?

☐ What three forms of proof will you use to structure your presentation and make it easier to recall?

☐ Which type of transitions will you use to guide your audience through your presentation?

CHAPTER 7

Corporate Storytelling

"Those who tell the stories rule the world."

—Plato, Greek Philosopher

We were on our way to Corpus Christi, Texas, to deliver a seminar for the Corpus Christi Hooks Baseball Club. The Hooks are the Double-A affiliate of the Houston Astros. We had been asked to speak to the stadium day-staff of 150 employees on the topic of communication in customer service leadership.

Since Corpus Christi is a four-hour drive from our corporate offices, we had time while driving to review our delivery for that evening. One question Kevin raised was, "What is our opening story going to be?" While we had both prepared for our segments of the delivery, we had not settled on how we were going to specifically open the entire session. One of us offered the idea of doing something related to baseball. We discussed how a baseball story would connect with the audience, but it was not tied directly to the key point that customer service can create fans for life. Then a story about one of our vendors, Document Engine,[1] was suggested.

They print and assemble our entire workshop curriculum and always do a fantastic job. In one instance, we had a rush order from a new customer of ours and Document Engine produced the curriculum in a matter of hours. Then, Andy Combs, the founder and president, dropped off the finished product at Kevin's house that evening so he would have the materials to take to our customer first thing in the morning.

So that is the story we decided to use to open the seminar that evening. It pointed directly to the power of amazing customer service with attention to the details. It was a story they could all relate to at the ballpark, given the importance of their attention to detail in how they greet the fans, how they help them locate a seat, and how they serve them a cold drink.

 Kevin's delivery of the Document Engine Story
http://www.CorporateOvations.com/kevinstory

Our life is our story. People relate to stories. People connect with stories. For centuries, history was passed down through the generations using stories. Just because we have so many recording devices, news media and historians doesn't mean that we don't use stories anymore, because we do.

Think back to any history class you have taken. Usually people either loved taking history or they hated it. Those who hated it tended to think about it in terms of having to memorize dates, names, and facts. We agree that memorizing statistics is quite boring. The people who absolutely loved history look at it differently. They look at history for what it truly is, a story unfolding in front of them. They see human characters, the plot, the tension, the struggle, the conflict, and the solution.

Everyone loves a good story. If you want to connect to your audience, don't just give them a bunch of statistics, give them the story. The hardest part about using stories effectively is making sure they are simple—and they reflect your core message.[2]

> "If you want to change the world,
> you need to change your story."[3]
> —**Michael Margolis**, Speaker, Coach, and Author

In a corporate environment, the higher you rise in an organization, the more you need to be skilled at storytelling. When a senior leader speaks to her team, a financial executive speaks to Wall Street, a business development manager speaks to a prospect, or a CEO speaks to his company, they need to have the skills to share a vision through a story.

Where Do You Start?

The first question you need to ask yourself is, "What's the point?" Why do you want to tell a story? What is the point you want to make with your audience? Once you understand the point you want to make, you can look further into what type of story you will deliver.

For example, if your team is being faced with a large obstacle that seems insurmountable, you want to make the point that if you focus on the goal and work together, you can overcome any obstacle. Or perhaps your audience needs to focus on providing exceptional customer service because doing so will have long-term benefits for your entire organization. Think of the point as the moral of the story. Why are you telling it? What do you want your audience to take away from it?

The first step in developing your story is to identify the key point. Once you have documented the point you want to make, you can now look for the story.

> "Storytelling is the most powerful way to put ideas into the world today."
> —**Robert McAfee Brown,** Theologian, Activist, and Author

Where Can You Find Your Stories?

One attendee at a workshop asked us if it is okay to make up a story. Our short answer to that is, "No, not if you are portraying them as truth." And really there is no need to make up stories because there are tons of stories all around you and more are being created every day.

You can get your stories from television, theater, books, the web (always check the source!), media, other people, and of course, your own life. While there are many sources for you to observe and research for stories, none will be more popular with your audience than your own stories. We can't tell you how many times we hear a workshop attendee say, "I don't have any stories to tell." That just isn't true. It doesn't take climbing Mt. Everest or swimming the English Channel to make a great story. Everyone has stories to tell because everyone lives a story every day.

A great example of taking everyday life and making it interesting is the show *Seinfeld*. This popular situational comedy aired on NBC for nine years for a total of 180 episodes.[4] Whether you watched the show or not, it provides a lesson we can all learn about storytelling. *Seinfeld* (and even the *Jerry* show pitched to NBC in the *Seinfeld* show) was touted as a show about *nothing*. But really it wasn't about nothing, it was about everyday life.

Jerry Seinfeld had a way of looking at everyday life through a different lens. When he invited his audience to join him in looking at a normal situation through that lens, we found it comical. Another comical storyteller is Bill Cosby. Bill Cosby never told jokes; he simply told us stories with a different perspective. Both Cosby and Seinfeld give us stories about their own lives, through their own unique viewpoints.

> "One of the most important things
> to keep in mind using stories in organizations
> is to get clear, and stay clear, on the purpose
> for which the story is being used."[5]
>
> —**Steve Denning,** Leadership Expert and Author

We are not saying that your stories need to be comical masterpieces to connect with your audience. These examples just show us that our everyday life is a story waiting to be told. Start observing your own life and documenting stories. If you want to get more serious about capturing your stories, use an audio recording device to document your stories as they happen, or carry a journal to write down the stories of your life.

Look for the message in the stories of your life. Then record them for future use. To keep up with our stories, we both maintain a document on our laptops. Every time we experience a story that could be used in a future presentation, we record it in that document. These stories include confrontations while traveling for business, incidents on family vacations, and interactions with people at the office.

One of our favorite questions to ask when we have dinner with a new contact before a speaking engagement is, "So, what's your story?" What if they answered this question by saying, "I was born on May 25, 1971, in Austin, Texas. I went to elementary school at Voigt Elementary, middle school at C.D. Fulkes, and then attended Round Rock High School. I married Lisa Benson on April 15, 1992 . . ." How interesting is this story? Are you going to remember this? Does it tell you anything about who this person is? (Other than the fact that they are an exceptional bore when it comes to conversation!)

In a research study[6] a text was given to a group of subjects. Later, the subjects were asked to recall the information as best they could. The subjects found certain sentences much more interesting, and they were able to recall much more when the sentences were both concrete (not abstract) and familiar.

What does this study tell us? It tells us that we store information better when we can relate to the content. If we understand it and it is familiar, we are more likely to internalize the information. Understand that when you provide a story, the audience will process and store it for later even if they don't remember all the words you specifically used in the story. They will hang on to the stories that make sense of the content. They will hold those stories that they can relate to, the stories that are familiar.

In response to the question, "What's your story?" we want to hear the concrete meaning of the story that can only be qualified as uniquely *you*. Everyone lives a story and everyone has a story to tell. We learn more about a person when we hear their story, not just the facts of their life. It provides us with a way to relate to that person. Start recording the stories of your life today. Your audience wants to hear them because your audience wants to know you.

> "Stories are the emotional glue
> that connects an audience to your idea."
> —**Nancy Duarte**, Writer and Graphic Designer

How Do You Select the Right Story?

So you know the point you want to make and you have found two potential stories you could use to support your key point. Your key point is that you must trust others and be willing to take a risk if the team is going to succeed. One story is from your personal life and one is from historical figure and author, C.S. Lewis. Both stories can be told in two minutes and both support your goal for developing trust among the team members in your audience.

Your audience is a group of 20-somethings who just joined your company as their first professional job after graduating from college. Your story took place when you were approximately 28 years old and you received your first professional promotion from the role of a project manager to a project team lead. In your new role, you took too much on your plate because you wanted everything done your way. You had been promoted because you were a good worker, but now you found yourself doing everyone's work plus your own. You began to think management was more headache than harmony.

Your C.S. Lewis story is one of him having lunch with J.R.R. Tolkien as they discussed each other's fantasy books, the The Chronicles of Narnia series and the Lord of the Rings series. Tolkien sharply criticized the Narnia series.[7] C.S. Lewis could have walked away from the project, but he trusted his friend was speaking to him in truth. Tolkien was not trying to hold Lewis back. He was giving honest feedback to help improve the story. This allowed Lewis to face the criticism, but persist with writing the series. So, which story do you go with? Both can support a message of trust between peers, but will one of them land stronger with the audience?

> "We live in story like a fish lives in water.
> We cannot think without language;
> we cannot process experience without story."[8]
> —**Christina Baldwin,** Teacher, Facilitator, and Author

The decision on which story to select can be made by reviewing three critical factors: How much time do you have? What is the purpose of your presentation? Who is your audience?

The time is usually an easy factor to weigh. If you have a story that requires more of a set up and a conclusion to be told properly, you can quickly eliminate it if you have a short time to present. Most of your stories should be able to adjust to shorter or longer timeframes, but if not, this factor can eliminate some stories right away.

Second, look at the moral of your story. Is the moral or meaning strong and evident? Does the moral of the story support your overall goal and purpose for the presentation? When the moral of a story clearly supports the point you want to make and it further supports the overall purpose of your presentation, it is a strong candidate. Anytime you feel like you need to stretch a bit to make the connection between your story and the purpose of the presentation, you should consider eliminating or replacing the story.

The third and final factor to weigh when selecting a story is your audience. You have already done your audience analysis in Chapter 3. You know who they are and what they are expecting. Put yourself in the shoes of the audience and look at your stories. As a member of the audience, do you think one story would connect with you more than the other? Why? Don't just look at the story from your standpoint; look at it from the audience's viewpoint. Just because you like to *tell* a story doesn't mean every audience will want to *hear* that story.

In the example above, you are selecting between a personal story and a story about C.S. Lewis. If you decide the young audience is a group of go-getters, anxious to move up in the organization, your own life lesson may be the most effective with them. If you decide this young audience is energetic but untrusting of each other, you may choose to tell the story of C.S. Lewis.

At their age, *The Lord of the Rings* and *The Chronicles of Narnia* may be well known to them and may capture their attention as they picture dramatic scenes from the books (or more likely the movies). The ultimate goal is to select the story that will work to support your objective for speaking, will relate best to this audience, and fits in the time frame you've been given to speak.

Vijayaswari Rajendran, a buyer for Cameron International Malaysia Systems,[9] demonstrated this perfectly in one of our workshops as she was preparing a presentation to a group of potential vendors who were interested in working with her company:

> Our procurement team went to a local restaurant for dinner last week," she told. "The food was outstanding—some of the most authentic cuisine we've ever had. The prices were unbelievable—excellent value for the money we spent. The only issue we encountered in what otherwise would have been a perfect evening . . . was the 45-minute wait for the food after our order was placed. And because of the delay, we will not be dining at that restaurant again.
>
> Our experience at this restaurant is no different from how we deal with our suppliers. You can have outstanding products—we settle for nothing but the best quality. You can have great prices—we expect to get a great value for our large volume purchases. But if the delivery of your products and services cannot meet the needs of our manufacturing plants, we simply cannot do business with you.

What Are the Elements of a Good Story?

The difference between a story and the other examples (like illustrations and metaphors) you learned about in Chapter 4 is the model. Stories have a distinct model or template for their construction. All stories contain characters. Sometimes they're human. Sometimes they're animals or insects (horse, dog, butterfly). Sometimes they're even inanimate objects (a tree, a rock, a fencepost). There is usually one main character in the center of the action. The main character can be you (the speaker), a friend, a rock, a dog, or even a group or team.

Every story has some form of action taking place. If there is no action, then there is no story. And in that action, the main character faces a dilemma. It can be a struggle they need to overcome or a choice that needs to be made. Whatever it is, the dilemma will create tension in the story. This tension can range from deep and philosophical to shallow and humorous. Either way, the situation must be resolved for the story to end satisfactorily for the audience.

Your audience wants all the loose ends tied up. They want to see resolution. This is no different than watching a murder mystery movie and feeling cheated when the movie ends and they never told you what happened to the bloody knife in the kitchen! Bring resolution to your story to generate a healthy response from your audience. The resolution provides the audience with the tension relief and a moral that can be applied to their learning.

> "The human species thinks in metaphors
> and learns through stories."
> —**Mary Catherine Bateson**, Anthropologist and Author

How Do You Deliver the Story?

If you are a *Seinfeld* fan, we have a question for you: Did you ever try to replay some of the show's comical lines to your co-workers on Friday while standing around the water cooler? If so, you probably didn't always get the same response *Seinfeld* generated from his audience.

Knowing a good story and *telling* a good story are two different things. Effective storytelling takes practice and rehearsal. After you tell a story, request feedback from a trusted peer so you can refine the delivery of your story. What are some of the areas you can focus on when rehearsing and refining your stories? There are several:

"A story has its purpose and its path.
It must be told correctly for it to be understood."
—Marcus Sedgwick, Illustrator, Musician, and Author

Use Characters to Bring the Story to Life

The characters in your stories are the main focus. If your main characters are people, give them names. If it's an embarrassing story for the character, change the name to protect the innocent (like the fine print at the end of a movie that says, "Any resemblance to real persons, living or dead, is purely coincidental"). Names for characters make the story come to life. We are able to relate to the characters better when they have a name.

If you are speaking about a company as the main character, use the company name, if you have permission. In any setting, you never want to use a person or company name if it will paint that character in a negative light. For example, if we had worked with a Fortune 500 executive with an abysmal attitude and speaking ability, we would never share that person's name or the company's name. Our point here is this; use character names to bring your story to life, but also use common sense to avoid slander!

Knowing a good story and telling a
good story are two different things.

Give the Story a Voice

When you sit down to read to your kids (grandkids, nieces or nephews), what's the first thing you usually hear from them? "Do the voices! Do the voices!" right? Adults are no different from children. We want to hear the dialogue as if it is real dialogue. In other words, don't tell your story like this:

"Then Barry told the team they should make changes to the program before it is too late."

Tell it like this:

"Barry demanded, "You *all* need to make immediate changes to the delivery of this program! If you don't . . . this program is done."

Now this doesn't mean you need to take an acting class so you can deliver your dialogue with drama and feeling, it just means that the audience wants to hear the dialogue as if it is unfolding in front of them in real time. Do you notice how the first example sounds like the past tense? Barry has already spoken to the team and now the speaker is telling the audience what happened on that day. It is almost like a sportscaster giving the recap of a game. Now look at the second example. Do you see how this example sounds like the story is actually unfolding right in front of us as if we are there watching it happen? Taking your audience into the present and into the action helps them create a more vivid picture of the story in their mind.

Another way to think about this is when you're listening to an audio book. The talented readers for audio books are able to deliver dialogue to us with different voices for each character. In the audio version of Steve Martin's autobiography, *Born Standing Up*,[10] Steve Martin reads the book to you. The power of the delivery is so much better than another person reading to you because when Martin describes a few jokes he used from the stage, he actually delivers them to you! In your mind's eye, it is as if you are sitting in the audience watching him perform.

The effect on the listener would not be nearly as powerful if another person were just reading those lines to you. As we listen to the drama and dialogue unfold in real time, we can actually picture the scene taking place right in front of us. This can differentiate between telling a *good* story and telling a *great* one.

Get Your Timing Right

In the next chapter you will learn more on developing *how* you say something using your voice. For now, let's focus on timing.

With comedy you may have heard the expression "timing is everything." Whether it is the timing of a one-liner or the timing of a pie to the face, timing can create powerful moments. If you share a story about giving your son a gift for his fourth birthday and taking him to Orlando, Florida . . . and Houston Astros' Spring Training!, you could generate a laugh from the audience if you pause after "Florida" just long enough so that everyone in the audience thinks "Disney!" before you drop the unexpected on them and say "Houston Astros' Spring Training!"

Besides the obvious use in comedy, timing can play a powerful role in your delivery to help the audience paint a picture in their mind. Mark Sanborn[11] is a talented professional speaker who is a master of timing in his delivery. In one story, Mark tells of being stuck in the Atlanta airport on a layover and accidentally answering his cell phone when he was calling his own number from a payphone. His timing is well rehearsed when he delivers the money line that gets the first of several laughs.

"I dial my cell phone into the payphone."
"My cell phone begins to ring."
"I think it must be Lisa."

He delivers all three of those lines in rapid succession because he knows that if he pauses after the word "ring," the entire audience will jump ahead in his story and start to laugh before he can say "I think it must be Lisa." If he were to deliver that third line after they are already laughing, it would be counterproductive because the audience would already know the punch line. He would be stating the obvious at that point and his story could potentially lose momentum. Understand that all audiences want variety from a speaker. Variety is welcomed and can help the audience pick up on the true meaning of the story. Rehearse the timing of your delivery with special focus on the areas where you should pause.

Mark Sanborn's Atlanta airport story
http://www.CorporateOvations.com/airport

Working on the timing for delivery is best done with the assistance of someone else. In our mind we often have a pace in mind for delivery, but others can listen and tell you when they felt like a line was rushed or held too long.

Use Your Body Language to Paint the Picture

When a story is delivered well, audiences can be transported through space and time as they watch a story unfold in front of them. We are not suggesting you turn your next speaking engagement into a Broadway production of *The Lion King*.[12] We are only asking you to consider what your hands, posture, feet and face are saying to the audience when you deliver a story. When the story comes from a talking mouth with no gestures whatsoever, the audience must work harder to build the picture in their mind. Simple hand gestures can help pull the audience into the story.

Body language helps bring a story to life.

For example, if you share this line in your story, "The phone began to ring and I was the only person there to answer it, 'Hello, this is Doug.' On the other end of the line was an irate customer who didn't receive their shipment by the promised date." What did you picture in your mind? How could you help reconstruct what you pictured in your mind if you were delivering that line from the stage? At a minimum, you probably picture picking up an imaginary phone and holding it to you ear, right? What about the person on the other end of the phone?

If you were just reading this example in the book, you had to read the entire example before you knew it was an upset customer. If you were speaking this story to the audience, how could you help your audience picture the story as it unfolds? Did you picture a screaming customer on the other end? If so, how would you portray this with body language?

Right after you placed the imaginary phone to your ear, you would most likely pull your head back and hand away because the screaming was hurting your ears! You might also grimace in your face as you realize the rest of the conversation is going to be difficult. Or maybe you put a look of regret on your face as you wish you had just let it go to voicemail. Body language in a story helps bring the story to life. How much body language you use will depend on what you are trying to achieve with this presentation (your purpose.) It will also depend on your audience. Are you speaking to senior executives about approving the budget or are you speaking to a group of new hires for the customer service call center? (In Chapter 9 you will learn more about the effective use of body language when speaking.)

"A story develops and grows in the mind of your listener. If it is a good story, you don't have to keep it alive by yourself. It is automatically retold or replayed in the minds of your listeners."[13]
—**Annette Simmons**, Speaker, Trainer, and Author

What Are Two Corporate Stories All Leaders Should Be Prepared to Share?

In the corporate world, we share stories all the time. As you move further up in an organization, stories become more prevalent because executives and senior managers make decisions at a more strategic level than a tactical level. In other words, big decisions are made and the lawyers, accountants, and front-line managers address all the details.

We're not saying that executives don't care about the details, the bottom line, margins, and ROI. But in addition to the bottom line, executives need to have a vision for the future. They need to see the story unfold. Executives understand their role in the corporate story currently being written. This story needs to be told to the organization and it needs to become a reality. The characters in this story are all looking up to the executives. True leaders tell the untold story of the company; untold because it hasn't been written yet. Leaders must see the vision and then cast that vision. Casting the vision means they must tell the company story.

> "I realized the importance of having a story today is what really separates companies. People don't just wear our shoes; they tell our story."
> —**Blake Mycoskie,** CEO, Tom's Shoes

The Company Story

The first story all corporate leaders must be prepared to tell is the *Company* story. How did the company start? What does its future hold? Why does the company exist? What is the company mission? Leaders will be asked to share different versions of this story to different audiences on a regular basis. For each audience, there will need to be minor modifications to create a connection.

For example, a sales executive may tell the company history and vision story to her executive sales team at the annual sales conference. The purpose is to build momentum with the sales team as they take on new aggressive sales goals for the next year. If the sales executive is speaking to the executive management team of a current customer, she will adjust the history and vision story to connect directly with the customer. While the history lesson and the vision for the future doesn't change, the delivery should always be considered based on the purpose you are trying to achieve and the audience you are addressing.

> "Stories are the single most powerful weapon in a leader's arsenal."
>
> —**Howard Gardner**, Harvard University Professor

The "Who Am I?" Story

The second story for corporate leaders to master is the *"Who am I?"* story. At every level in the organization, people will ask you about *you*. If you are interviewing for a new role within the company or if you are taking over the management of a merged department, you will need to share your story.

As we said earlier, one of our favorite questions to ask when we meet new business contacts is, "What's your story?" Everyone has a story. Most of us have never practiced, rehearsed or even thought about how we would answer that question. Remember from our example earlier that learning history by memorizing dates and facts can be cumbersome and boring. Your story is no different. Don't provide the audience with a talking resume including every date and fact about your professional career, because that is cumbersome and boring. Give the audience your story.

In most cases when someone asks for your story, they don't want a 30-minute presentation on your past experiences. Using the suggestions and tools we delivered in this chapter, develop your story with characters, dialogue, struggles, and success. The audience wants to hear more about what makes you . . . you!

For example, a speaker could describe their experience to you like this, "I graduated in 1991 from college and went directly into the US Navy. I was a nuclear submarine engineer for three years. I left the Navy and moved into corporate sales for a computer chip manufacturer. Now I'm a manager of a sales team for that company." We learned about this person's experience and employment but only through facts and statistics, graduated 1991, three years on a submarine, sales for computer chip manufacturer, now sales manager.

What if the same person offered their story by *telling* a story? "My past experience involves three years on a nuclear submarine and now six years in corporate sales. Both positions have something in common, leadership in tough situations. Let me give you an example, when I was aboard the USS *Virginia* we were submerged at 800 meters when my radar told me we had an obstacle 4,000 meters in front of us . . ." Then, toward the end of this story, the author could tie this to corporate sales, understanding how to work a sales pipeline, and learning to navigate around obstacles in the sales process.

Keep in mind two things with this example, first, not everyone needs to tell a Tom Clancy[14] story to create an interesting story. Second, always be respectful of how much time you have to tell your story. In most cases, you should be able to share your story in one to two minutes. If it goes much longer, you may need a Tom Clancy plot to keep the audience interested.

"Over the years I have become convinced
that we learn best—and change—from hearing
stories that strike a chord within us. . . .
Those in leadership positions who fail to grasp
or use the power of stories risk failure
for their companies and for themselves."[15]
—John Kotter,
Harvard Business School Professor and Author

Everyone wants the story about you, not just the facts. Think about any job interview from your past. They already have your fact sheet (your resume) in front of them. When they meet you, they start asking you to share more about you. They ask you to tell your story. "So, tell me about yourself." Then after a few moments of information, usually centered on facts and data, the interviewer tries to dig deeper for your story with questions like, "It says you were located in Singapore for a couple years as part of a rotational program as an engineer for your company. Tell me more about that."

When they begin to piece together more about you, they realize they still need some of the blanks filled in to understand the real you. Then they start digging deeper with questions like, "Can you give me an example when you were required to take charge of a situation and lead a group?" Or they might say, "Give me an example when you had to call upon your creative skills to manage an issue to successful resolution." These questions are being asked because they need to know your story. Whether your audience is an interviewer, the sales team you lead, or an entire corporation, your audience always wants to know the real you. The only way they will get to know the real you is if you are able to share your story and connect with them.

Stories are not just for entertainment. Stories are the fabric of our lives. How we stitch the fabric together becomes the tapestry that is our life. Everyone loves stories when they are told well. Everyone has the ability to tell stories. It is a skill and it can always be improved. Capture your stories, practice your stories and share your stories. We will all be enriched by the experience.

—————— CHAPTER HIGHLIGHTS ——————

- If you want to connect to your audience, don't give them a bunch of statistics, give them the story.

- Start with these questions: "Why do you want to tell a story?" and "What is the point you want to make with your audience?"

- Everyone has stories to tell because everyone lives a story every day. Record your stories as they happen.

- Selecting the right story is dependent on three critical factors:

    1) How much time do you have?
    2) What is the purpose for your presentation?
    3) Who is your audience?

- All stories have characters, action, a dilemma, and a resolved ending. The resolution provides the audience with the tension relief and a moral that can be applied to their learning.

- Knowing a good story and telling a good story are two different things. Effective storytelling takes practice and rehearsal.

- The characters in your stories are the main focus. Use character names to bring your story to life.

- Audiences want to hear the story as if it is real dialogue; a scene unfolding in real time that we can actually picture taking place right in front of us.

- One key element of how you deliver a great story is timing. When well practiced, the right timing helps you create powerful moments with your audience.

- Consider what your hands, posture, feet and face are saying to the audience when you deliver a story.

- Every leader must be prepared to tell two types of corporate stories:
  1) The Company Story—The story of how the company started, where it is going, why it exists, and the company mission.
  2) The "Who am I?" Story—The story of you. Not just the facts of your life, but your life story—the story that provides the audience with the insight into the real you.

────────── **TOMORROW'S CHALLENGE** ──────────

As you prepare for your next presentation, answer these questions:

- ☐ How will you choose the right story to connect with your next audience?
- ☐ What techniques will you implement to bring your story to life?
- ☐ When will you document your "Company" and "Who am I?" stories?

CHAPTER 8

Say It Like You Mean It

"Talking is like playing on the harp;
there is as much in laying the hands on the strings
to stop their vibration as in twanging them
to bring out their music."

—Oliver Wendell Holmes, Sr.,
Physician, Professor and Author

We each have two kids, a boy and a girl. One thing that we share in common in our respective households is that the brother doesn't always get along with the sister. In fact, sometimes their arguments may lead to a minor scuffle which requires a breakup by one of the referees (parents).

Let's assume that we saw the whole thing start and it was the younger sister's fault; she started the whole thing. Our typical direction may be, "Young lady . . . you get over here right now and apologize to your brother." After the long stare with the disappointed look of abandonment on her face, she stomps into position directly in front of her brother. With arms crossed tightly, a wrinkle to her nose and a furl to her brow, she delivers one final stomp as she blurts out, "I'm sorry!" As you picture this scene unfolding and think about the final line of dialogue, we have one question for you . . . do you think she is *really* sorry? We'll come back to this, but keep thinking about it as you read on.

We use three mediums to communicate our messages to another person. They are visual, verbal and vocal. Communicating effectively involves what words we say (verbal), how we say each word (vocal), and what we visually portray when we deliver the message (visual).

Mixed Messages

Many of you may be familiar with the statistics from Dr. Albert Mehrabian's research at UCLA in 1967.[1] He specifically studied something referred to as *mixed messages* when communicating feelings and attitudes. His study broke down communication into the three basic channels of visual, verbal and vocal. A mixed message is when one of the three channels is sending a different signal out of alignment with the other two channels. If you send a mixed message when you are speaking, the three channels of communication are not all sending the same message.

Dr. Mehrabian discovered that each channel of communication (visual, verbal and vocal) actually carries a different weight with respect to how it impacts the interpretation of a mixed message. For example, this ambiguity can be created by you speaking words crafted to sound intelligent and convincing, but your facial expressions are telling a story of complete ignorance. Based on Dr. Mehrabian's study, the audience would most likely interpret the visual portrayal of ignorance as the real story.

When these mixed messages were sent to the subjects, Dr. Mehrabian found that 7 percent of the time the words that were spoken (verbal) were viewed as the true meaning. Thirty-eight percent of the time, interpretations were attributed to how (vocal) the message was spoken. The majority of the interpretations, 55 percent, derived the true meaning of the communication by what the recipient saw (visual) as they received the communication.

> "When you are communicating about important emotional topics, or while you attempt to persuade your audience of something, your voice, gestures, postures and movements take on extreme importance."[2]
>
> **—Dr. Albert Mehrabian,**
> UCLA Professor Emeritus of Psychology

While there have been many discussions and even misinterpretations created by Dr. Mehrabian's work, we can interpret two lessons from his research. First, each communication channel carries a different weight with regard to the believability of a message. The strongest weight is usually the visual. Second, if just one of these communication channels sends a different message from the other two, the message creates ambiguity and anxiety, forcing the recipient to choose which channel to believe—the visual, the verbal or the vocal. For the greatest communication impact, it becomes logical that sending congruent messages with each of the three communication channels is the best choice to avoid ambiguity and anxiety with the audience.

A social psychologist, Michael Argyle, expanded on Dr. Mehrabian's work by reproducing the experiment with subjects delivering more than just a single word as the communication. In his studies, longer passages of text were acted out using neutral, positive and negative tones. His methodology was more complicated than Dr. Mehrabian's but his also led to the conclusion that nonverbal channels are more powerful. In fact, he found that the nonverbal channels were 12.5 times more powerful in communicating interpersonal attitudes and feelings than the verbal channel.[3]

"Effective communication is
20 percent what you know and
80 percent how you feel about what you know."
—**Jim Rohn**, Entrepreneur, Motivational Speaker, and Author

Now go back to our story about the younger sister apologizing to the older brother. Did she say the right words? She did! She said, "I'm sorry." How about her tone of voice . . . did it sound sincerely sorry? No, not at all. What did her body language look like? Did she look sincerely sorry? Not at all. Do you see how one channel is sending the correct message by saying, "I'm sorry," but the other two channels are sending quite the opposite message of "I'm really not sorry at all and when Dad turns around I'm gonna do it again!" Is her message of feelings and attitude believable? No, it isn't.

In business settings, like many other situations, the discrepancies between the three channels are usually not so obvious. The good news is that each of us has been programmed since birth to look for alignment between the three channels. If someone is not being sincere with us, we can usually pick up on that in the communication. When you are speaking to an audience, they will be able to pick up on that too. That's why it is important for you to calibrate your three channels as you present to your audience.

The other piece of good news is that your brain *wants* to calibrate your channels. The problem begins when you present and you are not properly prepared. That's when fear and anxiety take hold. You become nervous. You are so focused on remembering content or trying to figure out what to say next that you will mentally get in your own way. You get in the way of your own brain!

As the brain tries to naturally align your facial expressions and vocal tones with the words you are saying, the logical part of the brain takes control and tells the brain to focus on what you are going to say next. When this happens, you appear nervous, unprepared, not confident, and completely out of your element. This is when you suddenly can't figure out where to stand, what to do with your hands, or how much you should emphasize your voice or slow your pace. No audience wants to watch that train wreck.

Even though you may be saying the right words, if you don't say it like you mean it, no one is going to believe you. In boardroom conversations or when presenting to a large audience, what you say must be believed to have impact.[4]

In this chapter we will focus on two of the three channels you use to create impact—the verbal (what you say) and the vocal (how you say it). The next chapter will focus exculsively on the third channel, body language.

Verbal—What you say

There is a reason why the professional career of "Speech Writer" exists. It's because the words you speak when delivering a speech or presentation are important! We all know that if you say the wrong word at the wrong time it can completely change the meaning of a sentence.

In ancient Greece there were four different words used for the modern day English word "love."[5] Today you might say that you love tacos, but you can also love your spouse. How can this one word have two incredibly different levels of meaning?

Using more exact, descriptive words can create a much stronger impact on our audience.[6] Presenters who understand this take the time to meticulously craft important areas of a speech, like the opening and closing, word for word.

> "The difference between the right word and the almost right word is the difference between lightning and the lightning bug."
> —**Mark Twain**, Humorist and Author

So what kinds of words should I use in my presentations?

As you speak, delivering your message using descriptive words can add to both your credibility and the attention of the audience. We're all familiar with great storytellers in our life. These people use descriptive words to paint a movie for us to watch in our mind. We get so caught up in the moment that we feel as if we have not only heard something, but have actually experienced it as well.

There are over 1,000,000 words in the English language.[7] The more words you know, the easier it is to create word pictures for your audiences. You can expand your own vocabulary in several ways. By reading or listening to books you will add new words to your word arsenal consistently. If you ever hear or read a word you do not understand, take the time to look up the meaning of the word. It will be useless to you in the future if you are not willing to invest the time to add it to your own vocabulary.

The Pros and Cons of Using Names

In his book *How to Win Friends and Influence People*[8] Dale Carnegie writes that a person's name is the sweetest sound to their ears. What this should tell us is that a person's name is precious to that person. In other words, we need to use names and use them properly.

When someone overuses your name and they don't know you very well, it can seem rude or at the very least, make you uncomfortable. For example, let's say Kevin was about to sit down for dinner with his family and against his better judgment, he answered the phone without checking the caller ID. On the other end he heard, "Hi, may I speak to Kevin Karschnik?" To which, he answered, "This is he." Knowing full well that he was about to be pitched something that he surely did not want to buy; he began to listen to the salesman's pitch.

"Hi there, Kevin, this is Dave with Lifetime Light bulbs. And, Kevin, we've got an over shipment of our light bulbs that just arrived and, Kevin, I've been authorized to call a limited number of people to offer them 50 percent off, Kevin! Now, let me also tell you, Kevin, that these light bulbs are guaranteed for life, Kevin. If they ever burn out we will replace them for you, Kevin . . ." At this point anyone would want to reach through the phone and grab "Dave" by the collar and tell him in a good Clint Eastwood voice, "Stop . . . saying . . . my name."

Admit it, you would be thinking, "You don't know me. I know you don't know me. You know that you don't know me. In fact, you probably know that I know that you don't know me . . . so stop saying my name, LIKE YOU KNOW ME!" Speaking someone's name to them can be considered persuasive, but it is a double-edged sword that can cause other issues. It is important to use people's names, but it is most important to use them properly!

It is important to use people's names,
but it is most important to use them properly!

When you are presenting to an audience of one or one thousand, if you can mention someone in the audience by name, it is not only appreciated by the recipient, it is also appreciated by the entire audience. We call this the halo effect.[9] When you connect with one person in the audience, three parties will appreciate you reaching out.

First, the person you reached for in the audience will feel directly connected to you. Since you called them by name, they will obviously feel a strong connection to you at that moment. Second, every person sitting around that individual will feel more connected to you. Assuming they know the person two seats away was just called by name by the speaker, they will also feel an indirect connection to you because your connection landed so close to them. Third, anyone in the audience associated with that person will feel more connected to you. They will be thinking to themselves, "Hey, I know that person!" As a result, they will feel an indirect connection to you, the speaker.

When audience members hear another audience member mentioned by name, it humanizes the speaker. Audiences want to know that the person speaking to them can relate to them. Calling people by name is one way to do that.

The Dangers of Weak Words

Choosing the right words and phrases can help build your intellectual image, the positive impression that audiences have of you and your trustworthiness.[10] While some words can increase the credibility of a speaker, other words can definitely take it away.

Weak words and phrases convey a sense of the speaker being unsure of himself. This is referred to as hedging in communication. Hedging your comments is when you refuse to take a strong stance on anything for fear of being incorrect. Therefore, speakers use words that keep their comments somewhere in the middle of everything. While it seems safe in this area, the audience interprets it as weak and not confident. Some weak words and phrases to avoid are:

- possibly
- basically
- maybe
- kind of
- sort of
- I think so

Any words that give the audience a sense of insecurity will take away from the credibility of the speaker. If the speaker is unwilling to stand firmly behind the topic they are presenting, the audience will have a difficult time buying into the message being delivered. If you don't believe what you're saying, why should the audience believe you? Strengthen your vocabulary with stronger, more confident words and phrases like:

- absolutely
- of course
- I am . . . , it is . . . , we are . . .
- definitely
- it will . . .
- certainly

Filler words add nothing to your
presentation; they only take away!

How Can I Eliminate Filler Words?

The number one word that must be addressed for all speakers is the filler word. Filler words most often show up as "um" or "uh" but anything can become a filler word depending on how it is used. Some people actually have a filler phrase instead of just a single word. One filler phrase that we hear more and more is "you know." Filler words and phrases tend to show up more when a person is nervous. Audiences will interpret numerous filler words to mean that you are unprepared and nervous.

With filler words the first question to ask is, "What should I replace my filler words with?" and the answer is nothing. Filler words add nothing to your presentation; they only take away! If they only reduce your credibility and add nothing, then we definitely want to eliminate them. They should be replaced with silence.

When a speaker is uncomfortable in front of an audience they will be uncomfortable with silence because they think it will be interpreted by the audience as a lack of knowledge. So, instead of allowing silence to fill the air, the speaker fills every silent void with the sound of their voice. As a result, the audience is subjected to this " . . . ummmmmmm." The incorrect logic of the speaker is "If I continue to make speaking noises then they will think that I'm well informed on what I want to say next." Unfortunately, this logic is completely flawed and it has the exact opposite effect on the audience. Filler words become a distraction and make the speaker look as if they are nervous and unprepared.

Now if filler words only take away from the power of the message, and they should be replaced with a pause or silence, the next question is the tough one. "How do I do that?" Eliminating filler words can be done in two simple steps. First, become aware whenever you use a filler word so you can catch yourself. Second, practice speaking out loud with no filler words. Let's look at these two steps in a little more detail.

Step One: Become Aware of Your Filler Words

Awareness is usually the first step to overcoming any type of challenging issue. Awareness of filler words can be done through recording yourself when you speak. With the improvements in technology over recent years and the increased prevalence of smartphones, the affordability of audio and video recording devices has now placed these devices in almost everyone's reach.

In fact, according to Forrester Research the estimate is that there will be one billion smartphones in the world by 2016.[11] Chances are, you will own one of those smartphones (in fact, you probably do already). And, if you have a smartphone, we know you most likely have an app for voice recording and possibly even a video recorder too. Take the time to record yourself and then review it. Listen to yourself speak and focus only on the filler words you hear. What are your filler words? How many times do you say them? When do you say them (i.e. when you are transitioning, collecting your thoughts, at the end of a question or sentence, etc.)?

If you don't have a recording device, recruit a trusted friend. Many years ago Russ wanted to overcome saying "um" when he was making sales phone calls. He recruited a friend to sit in the cubicle across from him for 30 minutes with a coffee mug and a spoon. Every time Russ said "um" while speaking on the phone, his friend would tap the mug. It was loud enough for Russ to hear, but not loud enough for the customer to hear. After hearing that "ting, ting" noise every time he said "um," he proceeded to make calls later that day without the aid of his friend. The first time he let the word "um" slip out, he heard a "ting" noise in his head. Once you become aware of it, you can begin to catch yourself and replace the filler word with silence.

Step Two: Practice Speaking Out Loud with No Filler Words

Overcoming filler words can be done through repetitive practice. Some people say, "Well, I would, but I just don't give presentations that often so I really don't have many opportunities to practice." One suggestion is to join Toastmasters International[12] to practice speaking and communicating on a regular basis.

But also understand that you are not limited to speaking from the podium. Eliminating filler words can be practiced anytime you speak out loud. Whether you are delivering a formal presentation or speaking in a casual conversation, filler words should be eliminated.

In our workshops, we coach participants to slow down and incorporate more pauses into their presentation. This technique helps them to think about what they want to say before the words come out of their mouth.

To practice speaking for extended periods of time with no filler words, one of the best exercises is to read out loud. If you have children to whom you read, this is a perfect opportunity. Not only will you get to spend time with your children, but you will also get practice speaking out loud with no filler words! When people read they don't say filler words. They just don't! There is no need to say a filler word because the words are right there in front of you.

If you will read out loud every day for five minutes, you can eliminate your filler words because your mind actually gets used to speaking without them. In addition, your ears get used to hearing you speak with no filler words. It now becomes much easier to catch yourself when you use filler words. Your ears will hear you speaking a filler word and your brain will say, "Hey! Wait a minute—we weren't talking like that yesterday when we were speaking out loud." Read out loud. It's a great way to train yourself to eliminate those fillers and the bonus is that reading, in general, will help improve your vocabulary.

> "It isn't what I say, but how I say it,
> and how I look when I do it and say it."
> —**Mae West,** Actress and Screenwriter

Vocal—How you say it

In theater arts, there is a difference between *reading* a line out loud and *delivering* a line. Seasoned actors will read their script and search their feelings to get into their role. For some roles, actors will research their character's lifestyles and actually place themselves in the same situations so they can uncover the feelings and thoughts the character is experiencing. It's an important part of the preparation process.

Once they understand the feelings of their character, they rehearse the delivery of their lines. We are not suggesting you take trips into the deep woods to find your inner feelings before each presentation, but understanding the thoughts and feelings of your audience will prepare you for the best vocal delivery for your presentation.

Picture this . . . your entire speech is typed on paper in a Courier 10-point font with no extra lines between paragraphs. It is several full pages of text, all in the same font and point size. Each paragraph has a justified alignment to make both right and left side of the paragraphs a smooth vertical line.

Now imagine that in the middle of a page there are two words that are vitally important for the audience to hear and remember. If we wanted to call their attention to these two words on the typed page, what might you do to draw attention to those words? You could **bold** the words, use *italics*, underline, change the font size, use a different font, change the color of the text, highlight the text, or type those words in ALL CAPS! Do you see how we use the tools of the word processor to draw the audience's attention to the typed text?

> "All the fun is in how you say a thing."
> —**Robert Frost**, Poet and Author

Now, picture that you are the word processor for a presentation or speech you deliver. How you speak the words to your audience will determine whether or not they sound any different. How you say them determines whether or not they notice those two words at all!

Think back to the methods we can use to draw attention to the typed text and answer this question, which method of formatting is the correct method? If you think about it, they are all the right method! Depending on the situation, the audience and the speaker's style, they could either bold it or change the color ... italics or underline.

Just like the word processor can format text many different ways to draw your attention, different speakers will choose to highlight their words differently depending on their style. For example, Robin Williams highlights his words differently than James Earl Jones because they each have their own style. Be the word processor for your audiences and give some thought to *how* you want to say what you're saying.

The *how you say it* is defined in four key areas—pacing, volume, inflections and silence. The use of these vocal tools provides the magnificent colors to the verbal canvas you paint for your audience. The command over voice is part of every professional speaker's toolbox.

James Earl Jones reading Mark Chapters 1 and 2 from The Bible
http://www.CorporateOvations.com/jonesbible

"The trouble with talking too fast is you may say something you haven't thought of yet."
—**Ann Landers,** Advice Columnist, *Chicago Sun-Times*

Pacing

The pace at which you speak will vary depending on your audience and the message you want your audience to receive. Think about this question: in most cases, when a novice speaker takes the platform and begins to speak, does the pace of their speech tend to speed up or slow down? I think we all know the answer to that one. In almost every case, the speaker's pace will speed up when they begin to talk. Why is that?

Well, in Chapter 1, we reviewed methods for overcoming the fear and anxiety people have with public speaking. In that discussion we reviewed the physical effects anxiety can have on an individual. The energy trapped inside from the increased adrenalin, endorphins, heart rate and blood pressure is bursting at the seams. When the speaker begins to speak, the floodgates have been opened! With an outpouring of energy, the words come flying out of the speaker's mouth at blistering speeds.

There is a time to speed up the pace and there is also a time to slow down the pace. But one thing is certain, the audience always wants to know the speaker is in total control. If the pacing adjustments look out of control, the speaker will look unprepared. The tension and anxiety will build in the audience as their confidence in the speaker begins to erode.

If you are in control when speaking, then you need to use faster or slower pacing effectively. Varied pace and tone indicates excitement and importance.[13] When would you want to increase the pace of your message? You may be thinking, "Maybe when you have a lot of material left and you're running out of time!" To that idea we are going to say, "No." You will see speakers use a faster pace when they are adding excitement to their message. The increased pace will often accompany an increase in volume. Both together tell the audience that this is an important topic or an exciting topic.

> "This is going to be our best quarter ever!" (spoken fast and with volume to create excitement)
>
> "It goes to management for approval, accounting for review, project management for planning, and operations for delivery." (spoken in a fast pace to create a tedious feeling)

When would you slow your delivery pace? When a topic is heavy or somber, we want to deliver it with weight and gravity. You will see many talented speakers slow their pace to draw attention to a vital comment; so vital that it may mean life or death. Slowing your pace allows the audience time to swallow and digest the message as it is being delivered. It gives them an opportunity to feel the weight of the message. In the next chapter, you will see how this technique can be combined with eye contact and slower body movements to create dramatic effects and memorable moments with the audience.

> "When we implement this strategy . . . we . . . will . . . not . . . fail!"
>
> "She made it as far as St. Louis. And that . . . is where her story . . . ends."
>
> "We must . . . approve . . . our budgets at these lower rates if . . . we expect to survive."

Delivering content at a dramatically slower pace might feel awkward at first. This technique needs to be rehearsed so the delivery sounds natural. Remember the importance of congruency in your delivery. If the pacing slows to create a strong impact with the audience but the body language looks completely hesitant, it will not have the desired effect on your audience.

Volume

"Speak to the back of the room." We assume you have heard this tidbit of wisdom before in reference to using the appropriate speaking volume. In one sense, it is correct. In another sense, it is too simplistic for the accomplished speaker. It is true you want to speak loud enough to be heard. Certainly, if you are without a microphone, your volume will determine whether or not others can hear you at all. The issue in larger rooms without a microphone is speaking loud enough to be heard in the back without speaking too loud to the front. If you find yourself in this situation, moving around the room during your presentation can provide all attendees an opportunity to hear you without being overpowered the entire time.

If you don't believe what you're saying,
why should the audience believe you?

Using volume as a tool for creating an audience effect can be used for both energy and gravity. Just as the pace will oftentimes speed up for a release of more energy, higher volume will usually accompany the quickened pace. The faster pace and louder volume delivers to the audience a shot of adrenalin and an exclamation point to make a topic more memorable.

If the topic being delivered is one of intensity or emotional importance, you will see speakers slow their pace and drop their volume to levels barely audible. This technique can draw just as much attention as the faster, higher volume delivery, but it creates a very different feeling in the audience. The feeling is one of weight, importance, seriousness, gravity or even sadness.

Speaking with the assistance of a microphone will create a greater range for the speaker's volume. The loud can get extremely loud and the silent can be just above a whisper, and yet still completely audible. Advanced speakers understand the importance of the range of volume to a powerful performance and they will always use a microphone when given the opportunity. If you are offered the option of using a microphone by the audiovisual coordinator for the event, the correct response is to always accept it. They know the room and the venue better than you. Trust their judgment. In addition, they are doing you a favor by providing you with the wide range of volume at your disposal.

Use all the tools at your disposal. Get comfortable with them. One final note on microphones, if you are able to make requests in advance of your speaking engagement, request the type of microphone you would like to use. The two microphones we find most effective to stage presenting are the clip-on lavalier (or lapel) microphone and the over-the-ear/head-worn microphone.

The hands-free wireless microphones allow you to move more freely with your delivery. If you ask for a wireless microphone without specifying hands-free, you may end up with a hand-held wireless microphone. This type of microphone will remove the use of one of your hands from your delivery. If you have not rehearsed with this type of microphone, it can make your delivery challenging. Regarding the technical type of microphone to use based on how it handles sound waves (cardioid vs. bidirectional, etc.), it is best to leave those decisions to the AV crew. That's why they get paid the big bucks.

> "I know that you believe you understand
> what you think I said, but I'm not sure you realize
> that what you heard is not what I meant."
> —**Robert McCloskey,** Illustrator and Author

Inflections

The inflections in your voice involve an adjustment to the pitch or the tone you use. Inflections applied to a simple statement can actually change the meaning of a sentence without changing the words. A change in inflection can appear as an emphasis on a word or syllable.

In our workshops, we will ask participants to practice *punching* certain words or phrases in their presentations. For example, read the following statement and place a different inflection or emphasis on the bold word each time you read it. By changing the inflection or punch on a different word each time, you can actually change the interpretation of the meaning.

I didn't say he was late. (Someone else actually said it!)

I didn't **say** he was late. (I may have written it, but I didn't say it!)

I didn't say **he** was late. (HE wasn't late . . . SHE was!)

I didn't say he was **late**. (He just didn't complete his work on time!)

Understand that the inflections in your voice play a huge part in the interpretation by your audience. Most speakers tend to spend more time thinking about *what* they are going to say and not enough time thinking about *how* they are going to say it.

One sales representative we both know does such a fantastic job using her voice over the phone; she is extremely successful when cold calling. Customers have told us, "I never listen to voicemails from salespeople and I absolutely never call salespeople back. But, for some reason, I listened to Dara's message from beginning to end and I actually called her back." When we asked the customer what it was in the message that made them want to call back, they said, "It wasn't what she said. It was *how* she said it. There was such a genuine passion and sincerity in her voice that I didn't feel like I was being given a sales pitch. I felt like a friend was calling and sharing some helpful information."

Amazing! All of that from how Dara used her voice while speaking. When we asked Dara if she had rehearsed her inflections and delivery, she said, "No, of course not. I really am passionate about the services we offer because I see how it changes people's lives. I also know we are not the best fit for everyone and I never force that. If they have a need we can service, I know we will knock their socks off. I guess that is where the sincerity comes from."

As a speaker, you know your audience is evaluating you from that first impression. We want you to be confident and look confident. One way to show that confidence is in your voice. For your statements to sound confident, it is vital that the inflection in your voice remains consistent or even drops slightly at the end of the statement. If the pitch of your voice rises at the end of a statement, it will sound as if you are asking a question.

Read the following statement out loud two times. The first time you read it out loud let the pitch in your voice go up as you say the "four-thirty." You will notice that your statement sounds like a question, as if you are asking the audience when the session is over.

"The workshop ends today at *four-thirty*."

Now read the statement again. This time let the pitch in your voice stay the same or even drop slightly as you say "four-thirty." You will hear that it sounds like a confident statement instead of a question. To show your confidence in your subject, it is important to maintain a static tone or drop your inflection at the end of your conclusion statements. Do not allow your inflection to rise if you are making a statement. When you speak, the pitch and the tone of your voice can communicate meaning more strongly than the words themselves. Using inflections properly will not only prevent a misinterpretation of your message, it will provide a more powerful and memorable experience for your audience.

> "It's not so much knowing
> when to speak, when to pause . . ."
>
> **—Jack Benny,** Comedian and Actor

Silence

Captivating to all audiences . . . is the power of the pause. Ask any professional speaker for the most important skills a professional speaker should master and we are willing to bet these two will be given to you every time—storytelling and the pause.

Of course, the storytelling skill was covered in Chapter 7. Compared to storytelling mastering a pause probably sounds easy. On the contrary, effective pauses can be one of the most difficult skills for a speaker to master. Why is that? It is because a lack of confidence in a speaker's own ability will cause an abnormal fear of being silent when on the stage.[14]

The speaker's fear usually comes from the false belief that silence will be interpreted by the audience as a lack of knowledge or preparation. As a result, mere seconds of silence on the stage can feel like an eternity when all eyes are locked on you. But to your audience it is a microsecond—a microsecond that punctuates the sentence, builds audience anticipation and improves the listener understanding.[15] The fear of silence *must* be overcome (see Chapter 1) if you want to take full advantage of one of the strongest tools any speaker can have.

A lack of confidence in a speaker's own
ability will cause an abnormal fear of
being silent when on the stage.

Pauses in speech are as important as the rests in music. What would music sound like if there were no rests between notes or between measures? The music would sound like noise! Pauses in speaking are very similar. Pauses create more of a tapestry of sound rather than non-stop noise coming from the speaker.

Pause After a Question
An excellent location to offer a pause to the audience is after a question. In fact, if the speaker does not offer a pause after a question, the question will lose its effectiveness. To truly engage the

audience with a question, the speaker must give the audience time to think about an answer. If the speaker asks a question and then immediately follows with an answer, the message sent to the audience is, "Hey everyone, I'm going to ask a few questions during my presentation today but they are definitely rhetorical and you don't have to answer them. You don't even really have to listen to the questions or think about the answers because I'm going to give you the answer right after the question anyway. In fact, if you'd like to go ahead and take a nap now, I am not going to expect anything from you during this presentation."

We are exaggerating just a bit, but it's true that if you ask a question to engage the audience, and then give them time to think and use their brains before you give them the answer, they will be much more engaged. If you are wondering how long you should wait before you give the answer, the magic number is based on several factors, but an effective pause will vary from 1.5 to 3 seconds. If you pause longer than three seconds after a question, there is a good chance someone in the audience will shout out an answer because they think the question is not rhetorical and you are waiting for an answer before you continue! Depending on the depth of your question and the size of your audience, your pause after a question can fluctuate. According to Craig Valentine, professional speaker and speech coach, your pause after a question should be long enough for you to mentally answer the question in your head[16].

Pause as a Transition

Speakers will also use a pause as a segue to the next part of the presentation. This signals to the audience that one topic is completed and the new topic is beginning. The transitional pause can also be coupled with the speaker physically moving to a different part of the stage. Both the pause and the body movement provide the road sign to the audience, signaling a transition from the current topic and a start to the new one.

"The right word may be effective, but no word was ever as effective as a rightly timed pause."
—**Mark Twain,** Author and Humorist

Pause for Attention

You probably learned the effectiveness of this use of the pause in the fifth grade. If a teacher wanted to get your attention when you were busy passing notes to a friend in class, they would just stop talking and stare. Soon, the deafening silence would raise the eyes of everyone in the class back to the teacher. Not that you want to communicate the feeling of being scolded in elementary school to your audience, but a pause can be an effective method for grabbing the audience's attention.

These pauses are usually not impromptu, but choreographed. The intent of the speaker is to pull the audience in close for the delivery of an important message, not to be missed! When pausing for attention, once again, the magic amount of time to pause will vary. In most cases, a three-second pause will be enough, but understand that it can vary. Once you hit the three-second threshold, the audience will begin to experience a growing anxiety. The speaker creates more tension in the audience the longer the silence persists.

If the intent is to create anxiety and tension, then continue with silence well beyond the three-second threshold. If that is not your intent, then we recommend you pause for a solid two- or three-second count before speaking again. Watch your audience during the pause. Their body language can provide you with the clues for when to start speaking again.

Practice Your Verbal and Vocal Skills

One exercise we facilitate in our workshops is called the Quote Exercise. We distribute some famous (and some not-so-famous) quotes to our students to read and rehearse. Then, one at a time, each student stands and delivers the quote. We want the focus to be on *how* they are saying the quote. As we listen to the quote, we decide how we want to stretch this person. Then, we offer coaching and ask them to deliver the quote again.

We tell the participants our feedback is not always to make the delivery better, but different. If someone in the workshop is naturally loud and energetic on stage, we challenge this person to drop the tone of the quote down to a heart-felt moment with a loved one (think Rose Dawson Calvert from *Titanic*[17]). If someone is naturally timid on stage, we coach them to read the quote again as if they are the leader of a great army addressing their troops before battle (think William Wallace from *Braveheart*[18]).

In each example, we are stretching the students by challenging them to use the wide variety of vocal gifts they've been given. Each tool in your communication toolbox must be practiced if you expect to use them all well when speaking from the stage. This is an exercise you can practice on your own or with others. Challenge yourself to stretch your vocal capabilities so you can always say it like you mean it!

CHAPTER HIGHLIGHTS

- There are three mediums we use to communicate our messages to another person:
  1) What words we say (verbal)
  2) How we say each word (vocal)
  3) What body language we portray (visual)
- Sending congruent messages using each of the three communication channels is the best choice to avoid ambiguity and anxiety with the audience.
- The words you speak when delivering a presentation are important. Use descriptive words to paint a movie for us to watch in our mind.
- When used properly, a person's name is the sweetest sound to their ears. Reference someone in the audience by name for attention and connection.
- Avoid weak words and phrases like: possibly, basically, maybe, kind of, sort of, and I think so.
- Strengthen your vocabulary with stronger, more confident words and phrases like: absolutely, of course, I am, we are, definitely, it will, and certainly.
- Filler words are a distraction to your audience and will reduce your credibility as a speaker. Eliminating filler words can be done in two steps:
  1) Become aware of your filler words
  2) Practice speaking with no filler words by reading out loud every day
- There is a difference between *reading* a speech and *delivering* a presentation. You are the word processor for the presentation you deliver; format the words with your voice to bring it to life!

- Variety is the key to a successful presentation. Vary the pace, volume, and vocal inflections, depending on your audience and the message you want your audience to receive.

- One of the most important tools in a speaker's toolbox is the power of the pause! Pauses in a speech are as important as the rests in music. Three place to pause when presenting:

  1) Pause after a question
  2) Pause as a transition
  3) Pause for attention

─── TOMORROW'S CHALLENGE ───

As you prepare for your next presentation, answer these questions:

- ☐ How will you synchronize your verbal, vocal and visual delivery?

- ☐ What strong words will you add and which weak words will you eliminate?

- ☐ When will you practice the delivery, including pace, volume, inflection, and pauses?

CHAPTER 9

Engaging Body Language

"The most important thing in communication is to hear what isn't being said."

—Peter Drucker, Austrian Writer, Management Consultant and Author

Have you ever seen a speaker take the stage in a meek fashion? His arms are crossed in front of him as if he's trying to give himself a comforting hug. His feet shuffle toward the middle of the stage, but he quickly retreats to a lectern so he can hide himself from the audience. Then with his head tilted down and his eyes on the floor he announces in a timid voice, "Thank you . . . I'm, uhhh . . . very excited to be here with you all today."

Excited, really? He may have said the right words but his body language is telling a different story! While timidity may be comfortable for you, understand this, your audience is watching your body language, which adds to their interpretation of everything you are delivering.

Adults rely more heavily on vocal tone and body language (69 percent) than they do on the actual words spoken (31 percent).[1] When watching a speaker, audience members will subconsciously run through a series of questions in their minds. *Does the speaker look like they know what they are talking about? Does the speaker look confident? Does the speaker like us? Does the speaker's body language contradict the message being delivered? Does the speaker look approachable? Do I like this speaker?*

Three Reasons Why Body Language is So Important

As the speaker, your body language will tell a tale of its own. You need to make certain it is reinforcing your presentation and not contradicting it. A speaker must be seen as confident and in control, approachable and friendly, and most importantly, your body language must align with the rest of your message.

> "The single biggest problem with communication
> . . . is the illusion that it has been accomplished."
> —**George Bernard Shaw,** Irish Playwright

Confidence Communicates Competence

Every audience wants to know that their speaker is confident and in control. When a speaker looks nervous and unprepared, it creates anxiety in the audience. Just think back to the last really bad presentation you saw. Perhaps, a less-than-confident speaker fumbled with his notes and then proceeded to point with a nervous, shaky hand at his projected slides. At first, you probably felt sorry for him, and then gradually you felt anxiety build inside as you became more and more uncomfortable watching a disaster unfold in front of you.

If the speaker is obviously struggling, a voice inside your head begins to say, "Somebody do something! Can't they see this person needs help? Should I do something? Oh that poor guy! I hope he can get through this." Those anxious thoughts may seem like exaggerations after the fact, but when you're watching that uncomfortable presentation, they seem very legitimate.

On the other hand, when a speaker's body language conveys a message of confidence and power, the audience can relax in knowing that the speaker has the floor. You start to think, "This speaker is in control. I can relax and enjoy this message because this person knows what they're doing!"

Approachability Communicates Connection With Audience

The speaker needs to be seen as approachable, receptive and friendly. Imagine the strongest, most confident and powerful speaker you can imagine, but imagine that she doesn't have a receptive nature. He or she may come across as overly powerful or intimidating to the audience. If an audience is intimidated, they may mentally disconnect from the message. This happens because the audience sees the speaker as more threatening than friendly. Audience members feel like the speaker does not have their best interests in mind.

This becomes especially true when the speaker verges on contempt or seems condescending in how they are presenting their content. As a result, the audience gets a big "Nothing" when they ask themselves the question, "What's in this for me?" Without the proper body language, the speaker can begin to sound like she is speaking for herself instead of speaking for the audience.

When their movements make them seem aloof, arrogant or condescending, a speaker's body language will disconnect them from the audience. Maybe you've seen an expert speak who became disconnected from the audience because his body language and facial expressions were inappropriate. Maybe he failed to connect by not making eye contact, turned his back to the audience for extended periods of time, or even pointed an index finger at members of the audience. There may have been no denying he knew his stuff, but his facial expressions and body language gave off the impression that he didn't care much about the audience. In truth, he may have cared a lot about the audience. But unfortunately he found it difficult to convey his discoveries and ideas to the audience in a receptive manner. Every speaker must remember that through body language and facial expressions an initial connection can be made or lost with the audience.

Message Alignment Communicates Meaning

The speaker's body language needs to align with the message. This is accomplished through movement with purpose. As we discussed in the previous chapter, the human brain receives communication primarily through three channels—the visual, the verbal and the vocal. When all three channels send the same message, the message is interpreted as trustworthy, confident and true. We call this congruent communication.

Whether you are speaking to an audience of one or a thousand, you should always strive for congruent communication. If you send signals during a presentation causing one of your audiences' channels to receive a different message, it creates an internal struggle for them. This can lead to an opportunity for multiple different interpretations among audience members which will potentially confuse them and will certainly prevent them from properly understanding the message you're sending.

When little attention is given to ensuring the message is aligned with body language, a speaker will leave an audience asking questions about the true meaning of the delivered message. Depending on the interpretation by the audience, it can lead to some members enjoying the message, while others dislike it or are completely confused.

You will notice all three reasons for attention to body language point back to one thing: connecting with the audience. Never forget, as a speaker it is always about the audience and conveying a useful and effective message for them. Take the time to think about your body language before you rehearse and before you speak. Some of our students joke with us and say it sounds like stage choreography and in many ways, it is. The larger the stage and audience, the more choreography you will want to consider as you rehearse.

Regardless of your stage or audience size, you will want to consider your stage movements, hand gestures, and facial expressions, as you prepare for your delivery. One speaker who did a great job of incorporating stage, hands and face is Zig Ziglar.

Zig Ziglar delivering "Attitude Makes All the Difference"
http://www.CorporateOvations.com/zigattitude

Stance and Stage Movement

We both grew up in the *Brady Bunch* era of television and would watch it regularly in the afternoon after school. One episode that still stands out for both of us is when Marcia wanted to improve her posture and poise so she walked around the house balancing a book on her head.[2] We don't recommend walking around with a book on your head all the time, but you should think about how to take the stage, how to present yourself on the stage, and how you can always give positive energy to your audience.[3]

The confidence your audience wants from you can be delivered before you speak your first words. As we're sure you've heard many times before, first impressions matter most. And that's true of your audiences too. They'll judge you and rank your confidence level, energy, and credibility on a scale of 1 to 10 within the first few seconds.

Recall in Chapter 4 what we said about Gladwell's explanation of thin-slicing[4] and how we use it to make snap assessments of people and situations. Of course, given time that impression can always change, but have no doubt, your audience *will* make a snap assessment of you in the first few seconds of seeing you.

Some of our workshop attendees will argue with us and say, "My audience already knows me. I've worked with them for years. They made their first impression of me a long time ago! So this doesn't apply to me, right?" Wrong. If your audience knows you well, they will come to the presentation with a preconceived notion of your confidence, receptivity and your abilities. However, they'll still make a first impression of you as you take the stage.

For example, if you attended one of our workshops and as you entered on day one, we greeted you with a friendly smile, eye contact and a handshake while dressed in a clean suit, pressed shirt and sharp tie, you would make a first impression of us. Then, we take the stage for a presentation. And rather than being the confident, well-practiced speakers, you thought we would be based on that first impression, we come off as nervous and fidgety. Maybe we're talking over each other or struggling with the A/V part of our presentation. Of course, this is just an example. We hope to never have a presentation like that, but we use it to make the point that you can have a first impression of someone off the stage, but you'll make a completely new first impression of that person when they actually take the stage for a presentation. And the same goes for people who may already be familiar with you in your audiences.

> "What you do speaks so loud
> I cannot hear what you say."
> —**Ralph Waldo Emerson,** Essayist, Lecturer, and Poet

Taking the stage

As simple as it may sound, simply taking the stage is the first non-verbal message you send to your audience. What do you want that message to be? If it is a message of confidence, then the movement needs to be deliberate and purposeful. If your message is one of high energy, then the movement should be quick and energetic.

Think about the game show *The Price Is Right*, once hosted by Bob Barker and now by Drew Carey.[5] Can you visualize the audience members coming down to contestants' row when they hear their name called out? They're always filled with lots of energy. We are not promoting the notion that you should take the stage as if you just won a new washer and dryer as your emcee introduces you, but you get the idea.

That type of an entry tells the audience one thing, "I'm bringing it!" You are definitely full of energy and excitement. Whether you are speaking in a conference room or on a stage at the national sales convention, your entrance should be considered before you make it because it will send a message. What you bring to the stage is contagious to the audience, be it boredom or energy. Think about these questions:

- What do I want my audience's first impression to be for this presentation?
- How can I show the audience I am confident?
- How can I show the audience I am receptive to their comments, questions and opinions?
- How will I translate this non-verbal message with my movements and body language?

What you bring to the stage is contagious— whether it's boredom or energy.

Grounding Your Stance

Once in front of the room, your stance needs to become what we call *grounded*. We use this term to identify a solid stance with your feet movement limited to within the 18-inch-radius circle around you, usually referred to as your personal space.

If you are thinking to yourself, "But I like to move! And, audiences like to see movement!" we agree and we will provide guidance on movement later in this chapter. For now, let's start with how to deliver a presentation from a solid grounded stance.

Around you there are several concentric rings of space. Beginning at the touch level is your *intimate space*. Out to 18 inches, as a radius forming a circle around you is your *personal space*. Beyond that is the *social space* and the final ring is called *public space*.[6]

Picture yourself on the stage in front of the room with a personal space circle around your feet. We want you to stay in that circle until you are ready to move to a different grounded spot on the stage. One of the biggest issues we see with our students with foot movement is a rocking, or a step up and back, or a box step (almost like they were dancing). When feet are moving without any real reason for movement, the audience will interpret this as nervous energy. You will appear less confident, unprepared or just plain nervous.

We need you to ground your feet inside that personal space circle. While standing inside the circle, it is perfectly fine to turn your feet occasionally to maintain alignment with your body as you turn to different parts of your audience. If your shoulders turn to the left, it's natural to adjust your toes to point in that same direction.

We use a rule to help remember to bring your body in alignment as you rotate to face different parts of the audience. We call this rule *Eyes, Nose, Belly Button, Toes*. As a speaker turns their eyes and nose to face a different part of the audience, it will look more natural and confident if the torso (belly button) and the feet (toes) will turn to face that same direction. When the belly button faces your audience, whether its one person or 100, it shows you're interested in the conversation with them. If the belly button is pointed away from the person you are speaking to, it shows a lack of interest in the conversation.

How Can I Learn to Ground Myself?

So how do you ground your feet if they have a natural tendency to box step or move nervously? In our workshops we must first get you in control of your foot movement. We start by taking you back to ground zero. This means absolutely no foot movement is allowed.

If you struggle with foot movement and stepping uncontrollably, you can use one of the following techniques to ground yourself. Place a masking tape "X" on the floor or create an 18-inch-radius circle with string. Then, hold your feet in that location for your entire rehearsal. Or if the visual aid of the tape or string does not work, stand on a book. By placing yourself on a pedestal (even just a 1-inch-tall pedestal like a book), you can trigger your brain to know you are standing on something. For the entire three to five minutes of speaking, remain on your pedestal. If you still find yourself stepping off the book to move around, in extreme measures, you could stand on a chair. This should be a last resort and should only be attempted with several spotters. We don't need anyone uncontrollably stepping off of a 30-inch-high platform!

Once you can speak for three to five minutes without stepping or moving, we know you are in control of your feet. Now we can begin adding controlled movement back into your delivery. Earlier we mentioned that some of our workshop attendees debate with us on stance and say, "I like to move. That's just me!" Others contend by saying, "I think audiences want movement. Nobody wants a statue for a speaker!" While both of these may be true, uncontrolled movement without purpose will confuse the audience or convey a message of unprepared nervousness.

So, how do you move confidently? You do so with what we call movement with purpose. When the movements of your body language are in alignment with the message you are delivering, it will reinforce the message to the audience. Movement with purpose helps the audience understand and follow you throughout your presentation.

The most polished speakers in the world spend a great deal of time rehearsing their stance and their movements. It is a form of choreography for speakers. Every movement should have a purpose. The purpose should serve the audience by assisting in the reception and interpretation of the message from the speaker. We agree that all audiences want to see movement from their speaker. We just want to make sure the movement is purposeful and conveying the right message. Now let's dive deeper into how you can create purposeful movements.

Picking Your Spots

Before you begin to move on the stage, know where you are going. This sounds simple or like common sense, but most speakers won't think about this until they have started walking. Speakers feel the need to move their legs and their brain gives in to the request from the muscles in the legs.

As the speaker begins to move, he will begin an internal dialogue trying to determine where to stop walking. If the speaker can't quite find the comfortable spot for stopping, the movement has no purpose. As a result, the speaker seems to wander aimlessly until he finds a comfortable, safe place to stand. If he doesn't find that selected spot as comfortable or as safe as he hoped, the speaker may end up retreating to the position he started from as if he just realized he was quite uncomfortable being so far away from his home position.

If you have ever been to a play or a musical, did you ever notice the pieces of tape or the markers on the floor of the stage? In theater, these are called marks.[7] The actors know exactly where their marks are located for each of the lines they will be delivering. Their delivery is choreographed so their lines are delivered from the most appropriate location on the stage to create the feeling the director wants. When you are speaking or presenting, you are the director. Prior to your delivery, think about where you want to deliver the different portions of your presentation. The larger the stage, the more thought you should put into your movements.

Movement Into the Audience

In 1983, Journey was on their Frontiers Tour.[8] We both saw them in Austin, Texas, on July 5th. While we couldn't afford the luxury floor seats or front row seats, we were there . . . in the mezzanine. For rock bands, the one disadvantage to playing to a large crowd is that everyone in the audience wants to feel close to the band, but logistically that just isn't possible. And that was true for us at the Journey concert.

From our mezzanine level seats, the band definitely did not feel close up or connected to us. But during one song, Steve Perry, the lead singer, made his way to our side of the stage and pointed up to the mezzanine level where we were sitting. Of course everyone in the three sections surrounding us thought he was pointing directly at them. Today, with the help of technology, bands are creating more of an intimate experience for their audiences with stage runways into the audience, jumbo screens to show close ups of the singers, and floating scaffolding that swings out over the crowd.

While we may not be rock stars with pyrotechnic engineers to choreograph our presentations, the point is this: audiences like to feel connected to the speaker. As a speaker, respect the need for the audience to feel a connection with you. As you are selecting the spots you will move to, remember to select a couple spots that will move you closer into the audience.

Think about your presentation and decide when you will make that physical transition. For example, if you are presenting in a conference room and one of your 12 attendees is your senior engineer for the project you are reviewing, you could choreograph your movements to be standing next to your engineer as you transition into the segment of the presentation where you will compliment her and her team for their work.

When you are on a larger stage and you don't have time to choreograph all your movements, you can use a template for large stage movement. We call this template the *CLR (Center-Left-Right)*. This template gives you three grounded positions on the stage: one in the center, one on the left and one on the right.

The starting position or the power position will be at center stage. This will also be your finishing position. When you are grounded at this spot, you will be seen as confident and delivering yourself equally to the entire audience, as long as you use the *Eyes, Nose, Belly Button, Toes* rule for rotating and facing them.

At some point, you will want to move in closer to your audience members sitting near stage left. By taking one-half step back from your power position and then turning toward your left, you can make your way over to your stage left spot. At this location continue to use your body rotation while grounded, but focus on the audience on that side with your eye contact. When you are ready to transition to another spot, you will make your way back to the center-power position.

When moving away from the audience on your left side, it would be considered rude to turn your back on them as you walk away. Instead, take one and a half steps back, to back away from the audience while you are facing them. Then, turn and make a confident and purposeful walk back to center stage. When you are ready to move again, repeat the same process to move to the audience at stage right. When using this process, choreograph your movements so you start and finish at center stage. Also, take note of how many times you visit stage left and right. For larger stages and audiences like this, you want to visit each side the same number of times.

Transitional Movements

In Chapter 6 we gave suggestions on how to create transitions in the body of your presentation to make it easier for your audience to follow you. Along with verbal transitions, you can add spatial movements to coincide with the transition. For example, if you are going to present the three key reasons why we should invest in a new cloud based customer relationship management (CRM) system, you could make point number one while you move to a grounded spot on your far left. Then, for point number two, take a couple steps to your right and ground yourself again. Then for your third and final point, take a couple more steps to your right. After you have made your three key points, make your way back to center stage (power position) to wrap up your presentation with your prepared close.

Transitional movements help your audience follow along with your content. If you make it hard on your audience to follow, they will quit trying. By using transitional steps along with your transitional statements, the audience will easily follow the structure of your message.

If you make it hard on your audience
to follow, they will quit trying.

Posture and Stance

Your posture and your stance will speak to your audience by sending a message about your confidence and your comfort level on the stage. Whether you are speaking in a conference room or on a large stage, make sure you give some thought to how you stand. Practicing your stance in front of a mirror or in front of a trial audience can give you the feedback you need before you speak. Here we'll focus on two types of general stances used by speakers. Which stance you choose will depend on your purpose (what are you trying to achieve?) and your audience (who are you speaking to and what do they expect?).

The Formal Stance

Since we want to convey confidence as a speaker, our posture and stance should look confident and proud. To give you a visual, a soldier standing at full attention is a slight exaggeration of the desired stance we want. The feet should be slightly less than shoulder width apart with your toes pointing forward or just slightly outward. The back should be straight and not hunched over with your shoulders slightly back. Some refer to the shoulders back by saying put your chest out. Be careful not to exaggerate this part of the stance or it can look contrived. Finally, your chin should be up slightly to show confidence and strong eyes looking in alignment with your nose, belly button and toes.

In addition to all of this, the formal stance is uniquely noted by equal weight placed on each leg. With equal weight on each leg the hips should be parallel to the floor. You want to create a triangle, the most stable figure in geometry, with your whole body. The stability will make you appear poised. When your body is balanced your mind also becomes balanced. Given the mind/body relationship, a balanced stance helps you focus your ideas more clearly.[9] This stance is best suited for more formal environments and with an executive audience.

The Casual or Informal Stance

The casual stance creates a more relaxed atmosphere and an informal connection between the audience and the speaker. The most obvious differentiator with this type of stance is unequal weight placed on each leg. This unequal use of the legs will cause a slight tilt to the hips. This stance coupled with more casual hand gestures will give the audience the feeling that this is more of a conversation than a keynote or presentation. While this sounds desirable, keep in mind that a conversational tone may invite more interruptions and questions from the audience. If your intent is to hold all questions until the end, you may consider a more formal stance. This type of stance is most effective with smaller audiences, informal presentations, or informative (teaching) or entertaining presentations.

The Receiving Stance

While in a formal stance, the speaker can put his hands behind his back in a handcuffs type of pose. This hand gesture behind the back is usually interpreted by the audience as a non-confrontational appearance by the speaker. It is sometimes referred to as a receiving stance. However, be careful because if this pose is maintained for too long, it may be interpreted by the audience as weak or not confident. The most appropriate time for a speaker to use this stance is when he is listening to a question from the audience. As soon as the question has been received, the speaker should bring the hands out in front and use appropriate hand gestures when delivering the response.

The Superman® Stance

When a speaker places their hands on their hips it is referred to as the Superman® pose. This is an extremely confident look and should be used sparingly and with caution. If the speaker takes this pose too often during a delivery, their confidence may appear extremely high, but they can also come across as domineering, aggressive or condescending. In our workshops you will often see the facilitator take this pose when the group returns from break. The audience needs to settle down and turn their attention over to the facilitator again. This pose signals to the audience that it is the facilitator's turn to talk again.

The Resting or Waiting Stance

When the hands are down and placed in front of the speaker, this is a rest position. This is sometimes referred to as the fig leaf pose. Depending on the context of the message and the audience it can be interpreted as resting, receiving or showing a sign of weakness. This stance looks most appropriate when the speaker is on stage, but it is not his or her turn to talk right now. This stance can work well if the speaker is showing a video clip, waiting to be introduced, or on the side of the stage waiting for his or her turn to speak.

Hands and Gestures

The number one question we get on body language from our workshop attendees is, "What do I do with my hands!?" The short answer is movement with purpose.

Reread the first sentence of this paragraph and think about a speaker delivering that line to you. What do you picture her doing with her hands? "The number one question we get on body language . . ." Our guess is that you are picturing the speaker holding up her index finger in a number-one gesture. That is movement with purpose!

An added benefit of using hand gestures is that the very fact of moving your hands around helps you recall your talking points—the gestures help you access memory and language.[10]

Here is an exercise you can practice for hand gestures. Have someone read the following list of phrases out loud to you. For each phrase, show an appropriate hand gesture that would align with that phrase. It's just like charades!

- This will benefit the whole world.
- Not only for our past projects, but for the future projects as well.
- With the increases in revenues we will surpass our targets.
- We achieved success beyond our initial forecasts.
- We will review the project development, implementation and our results.
- Think about the words you are speaking.
- Open the borders to increase our customer base.
- We can place you in our Los Angeles or our New York data center.

After you've gone through the list once, stretch your skills by going through it again, but don't use the same hand gestures you did the first time. The more you practice getting your hands up and into the conversation, the more comfortable you will become in using them in front of your audience. Keep in mind when you are speaking to larger audiences that you may need to exaggerate your gestures so they can be seen from the back of the room.

When we have an attendee in our workshop that is extremely averse to using their hands, we will approach the transition to greater movements in phases. The first phase is to get them aware of their hands so they can be controlled. For someone who is averse to using their hands they will tend to have nervous, fidgeting movements with their hands or fingers. It may be a ring twist, wringing hands, or the wrist flips to show the palms of the hands.

While speaking for a few minutes, we lock their arms and hands straight down at their side. Once they are able to control extraneous movements with their hands, we can then integrate controlled movement. The second phase is to get them to use their hands in a small way. We do this by working on hand gestures in what we call the *torso theater*.

The torso theater is the box area from your neck down to your waistline and inside the shoulders. Simple hand gestures in this area get the speaker used to using their hands without making them feel too exposed to the audience. The third and final phase is what we call the *get big* phase. This is where we choreograph one movement to take the hands outside the shoulders. This is a natural progression for the speaker where they use larger gestures to get outside the torso theater with bigger movements. If you struggle with using your hands comfortably, approach the use of hand gestures with this phased approach.

Emphatic Gestures

Hand gestures can be used to bring energy and excitement to a presentation. If you win a huge victory you will immediately throw both of your hands up in the air. You see this in sports quite often. This is an example of an emphatic gesture. Depending on your purpose for speaking, your audience, and your style, these gestures will take on different looks. Avoid overly dramatic gestures. Your gestures should be aligned with the content of your message and they should be practiced to look natural as you deliver them.

Illustrative Gestures

"I caught a fish *this* big." Can you picture the speaker using his hands to illustrate this comment? Speakers use illustrative gestures when they want to demonstrate a point rather than just say it. For example, if the VP of Sales is speaking to the entire sales team and wants to challenge them to increase sales over the next quarter by 3 percent, she may place her thumb and index finger close together to illustrate what a small request she is making. If the CEO is speaking to Wall Street about the 3 percent cut in expenses made this past quarter, she may use both her left and right hand to show a huge gap that has been cut.

If you use illustrative hand gestures, remember that if you illustrate something in space, direction or area, you will need to go back to that same area or direction when you refer to it again. If you point to different areas each time you refer to something, it will confuse the audience. For example, if you point directly behind you when you say, "That is when we decided we should be going South!" you should mentally take note that North is now in front of you, East is to your right and West is to your left. For the rest of the presentation you should keep those directions. The consistency of the hand gestures will help the audience visualize your presentation. This is called anchoring.

Anchoring Gestures

At times you may choose to implement a technique called anchoring. This technique uses a gesture to anchor a topic of the presentation to a location. Once you have anchored a topic to a location, you can return to that location during your presentation and the audience will be reminded of what it means.

For example, in one of our workshops, we review a communication model and act out what takes place in your brain during this process. During the explanation we anchor a security guard to a specific spot on the floor or stage. Later in the workshop we mention how "Interpretations at this point become difficult because . . . what gets in the way?" and we point to that spot on the floor and the entire audience in unison says, "The security guard!"

Symbolic Gestures

We are blessed to be able to speak to audiences around the world. However, over the course of our international work, we have discovered, sometimes the hard way, that different hand gestures mean different things in different parts of the world. When it comes to symbolic hand gestures, you should definitely know your audience before using them.

A symbolic gesture might be a thumbs-up motion to show that everything is good. In the USA, the thumb and index finger touching to make a circle with the other three fingers extended is interpreted as "okay," as in "everything in just fine." In the Middle East, the "okay" symbol would not be met with such a positive response. In the United States we might gesture the number two by holding up our index finger and our middle finger. In the United Kingdom if you were to do the same especially with the knuckles pointed toward the audience, you may offend a few people. You can incorporate symbolic gestures into your delivery; just make sure you know your audience so you don't unknowingly offend or alienate your audience with a hand gesture.

Facial expressions

Psychologist Dr. Paul Ekman is noted for his career of work on emotions and facial expressions. In fact, his work was the inspiration for the TV series *Lie to Me* (2009–2011).[11] Dr. Ekman found that all individuals could read basic emotions through the facial expressions they saw. The ability to do this is something we are born with and not something we acquire.[12]

When speaking, your facial expressions will tell a story to the audience. If the facial expression is not congruent with the message you are speaking, the audience will interpret the delivery as insincere, not confident or just plain false. Two areas we focus on for body language are your confidence level and your receptiveness. Both of these can be accentuated with facial expressions.

> "Actions speak louder than words,
> and a smile says, 'I like you.
> You make me happy. I am glad to see you.'"[13]
>
> —**Dale Carnegie,** Speaker, Teacher, and Author of
> *The Quick and Easy Way to Effective Speaking*

The Smile

The facial expression that conveys to your audience that you are approachable is a simple, sincere, genuine smile. If you know that you have only a few seconds to make a first impression, your smile should be on your face as you take the stage. French anatomist Guillaume Duchenne performed research on emotions and smiles and found that a genuine smile typically lasts up to four seconds.[14] If it goes beyond the four seconds, it is most likely forced and is interpreted as insincere.

When you stand to speak, your smile needs to be genuine, not forced, and not nervous. Keep in mind that depending on where in the world you are speaking and who your audience is a smile may have negative interpretations. In some cultures smiling is a sign of being nervous or unsure. In other cultures, smiles are used to cover up difficult emotions.[15, 16] While in most Western cultures, the smile will be seen as warm and inviting.[17]

> "A smile is the shortest distance
> between two people."
> —**Victor Borge,** Danish Comedian and Pianist

Eye Contact

Audiences desire eye contact and the speaker should give it to them. By making eye contact you are letting the audience know that you are confident in your skills and knowledge. Since your eyes are the only part of your central nervous system that is in direct contact with another human being, eye contact literally connects mind-to-mind. When your eyes meet the eyes of your audience, you make a First Brain-to-First Brain connection.[18]

In a small audience, eye contact can be shared with each individual in the room. For much larger audiences, the speaker should cast a gaze and make eye contact in each direction of the room. This way everyone will feel like the speaker has looked directly at him or her. Remember our example earlier about Journey lead singer Steve Perry pointing at us in the Mezzanine section? Everyone in the three sections felt like he had looked directly at them even though he was really just looking in our general direction.

Of course, you have to be careful of how long you keep eye contact with someone. In larger audiences, if you lock eyes with someone for one second, they will know you just looked at them. If you lock eyes with someone for two seconds, they will start to feel the gaze. If you lock eyes for three seconds or more, the audience member will most likely break the eye contact and look away. At the three-second mark, the audience member will feel awkward.

As the audience size gets smaller, you can look into the audience member's eyes longer without it feeling awkward. For example, if you are speaking to an audience of one, it would be entirely appropriate for you to look at that person for half a minute or even longer as you are engaged in conversation. Keep in mind that just like the smile, eye contact can have different interpretations around the globe.

It Takes Practice

Whether you're an actor, a singer, a dancer or a speaker, delivering a message to an audience isn't easy. It takes practice. For speakers, one of the most profound areas of influence they can practice is their use of body language. In fact, mastering their body language is essential because so much of communication is delivered through the visual channel. It is unfortunate when speakers rely heavily on software tools as their primary visuals because their message can be conveyed much more powerfully and personally through the effective use of body language.[19]

——————— CHAPTER HIGHLIGHTS ———————

- Your body language is the most important communication factor when speaking to an audience because it adds to their interpretation of everything you are delivering. It helps you connect with your audience in three ways:
  - › They know that their speaker is confident and in control.
  - › They know that their speaker is approachable, receptive and friendly.
  - › They know your message is trustworthy, confident and true.
- Audiences will be judging you before you start speaking. Your body language will play an essential part in their first impression.
- Your power position starts by grounding your feet inside an 18-inch radius, serving as a means to appear confident and prepared in front of your audience. If necessary, place masking tape on the floor to help your feet remain in one location.
- When you turn your eyes and nose to face a different part of the audience, it will look more natural and confident if the torso (belly button) and the feet (toes) turn to face that same direction.
- Uncontrolled movement will confuse the audience or convey a message of unprepared nervousness. Movement with purpose assists the audience in the reception and interpretation of your message.
- Markers on the floor can help you choreograph movement with purpose, including movement into the audience and transitional movements.
- Your posture and your stance will speak to your audience by sending a message about your confidence and your comfort

level on the stage. Choosing the appropriate stance for your presentation will depend on you and your audience:

> › The Formal Stance
> › The Casual or Informal Stance
> › The Receiving Stance
> › The Superman® Stance
> › The Resting or Waiting Stance

- Movement with purpose not only applies to your feet, but also your hands. In order to reinforce your message to your audience, your hand gestures should be in alignment with the message you are delivering. Four different types of gestures are:

  > › Emphatic gestures—used to bring energy and excitement to a presentation
  > › Illustrative gestures—used to demonstrate the point rather than just say it
  > › Anchoring gestures—used to anchor a topic of the presentation to a location
  > › Symbolic gestures—used to represent a word or phrase instead of speaking it

- Your facial expressions will tell a story to the audience. If they are not congruent with the message you are speaking, the audience will interpret the delivery as insincere, not confident or just plain false.

- The facial expression that conveys to your audience that you are approachable is a simple, sincere, genuine smile. A genuine smile typically lasts up to four seconds.

- Eye contact with audience members will let them know you are confident in your skills and knowledge. It connects the speaker with the audience.

─────── **TOMORROW'S CHALLENGE** ───────

As you prepare for your next presentation, answer these questions:

- ☐ What will you do to ensure your body language is aligned with your verbal and vocal communication?

- ☐ Which types of stance or posture will you use to effectively convey your message?

- ☐ How will you use hand gestures to align and reinforce your message to the audience?

,

CHAPTER **10**

Using Visual Aids

*"Create your own visual style . . .
let it be unique for yourself and
yet identifiable for others."*

—Orson Welles, Actor, Director,
Writer, and Author

Kelly began the 30-minute presentation to her senior management team by directing their attention to the slide on the screen with her agenda. "Today I'd like to tell you about our direction for this region, the goals we've been handed down from corporate, our current status on each of them, our plans for moving toward the new goals, a review by department of current gaps and then finally wrap up with a brainstorming session on our first steps in each area." None of this was a surprise to her audience, because every single word she spoke was on her agenda slide . . . including "Today I'd like to tell you about."

Unfortunately, *death by PowerPoint*®1 is a common occurrence in the corporate world. According to a survey of our students, two of the most annoying characteristics of poor presentations are slides with too much text and speakers who read every single word on the slide to their audience.

Why is it when someone says "corporate presentation" it means "endless, wordy, and boring slides?" Slides are slides. Documents are documents. They aren't the same. Attempts to merge them result in what author and internationally acclaimed communications expert Garr Reynolds calls the *Slideument*.[2] The downside to using slides as visual aids is that most people break the basic rules of constructing and using effective slides.

"Visuals should be used to enhance
an audience's understanding of a concept,
not used as cue cards."
—William Krieger, Professional Speaker and Author

We have nothing against using slides as visual aids. We love visual aids. In fact, research supports the use of visual aids to enhance the learning experience for the audience. The US Department of Labor studied audience retention three days after an event. It found people retained 10 percent of what they heard from an oral presentation, 35 percent from a visual presentation, and 65 percent from a visual and oral presentation.[3]

According to the authors of *So Each May Learn: Integrating Learning Styles and Multiple Intelligences*, research suggests that if you teach content in a variety of ways (visual, auditory, kinesthetic) the learners have a much higher level of understanding and retention.[4] All of this research also supports the common phrase, "telling ain't training." In other words, if you want to effectively inform and ultimately persuade your audience, simply telling the audience may be the least effective and least memorable method. To increase understanding and retention, visual aids can certainly help.

While computer generated slides can be an effective form of visual aid (when used properly), it is important to understand and appreciate the other forms of visual aids as well. By blending different types of visual aids into your presentation, you can create a more favorable environment for audience engagement, retention and persuasion.

> "If you have to explain a visual aid,
> you're working backwards.
> A picture is supposed to be worth a thousand words,
> not generate another thousand words."[5]
> —**Alan Weiss,** Professional Speaker and Author

What Can You Use for a Visual Aid?

Sure, you can use a Microsoft PowerPoint® or Apple Keynote® slide as a visual aid, but what else could be effective? Rather than reading the following list and ranking them, think about how you could incorporate multiple types of visual aids into your presentation. Keep in mind that the right type will be based on your purpose, the audience and the situation.

Video Projected Slides

As noted above, the first thing to pop into most people's minds when they know they are going to develop a presentation is usually . . . slides! Yes, slides are visual aids, but remember you have other choices too. You can use a mixture of different types of visual aids to engage your audience. If you are going to use a slide deck, what should you keep in mind? The easiest rule to remember is that less is more[6]. You can make a great impact with a slide as a visual if you keep it simple. The usual rule we apply for text on a slide is called the *Six By Six Rule*; this means no more than six lines of six words for any slide (that's a total of no more than 36 words per slide).

A Prop

In a play, a prop is used by the actor to bring reality, clarity or expression to a scene. If you are old enough to remember the comedian Gallagher, you know what is about to happen when you see him pull out his favorite prop—a giant sledge hammer.[7]

In business presentations, a prop can be a stack of reports, a cell phone, a signed contract, a pen, a dollar bill, an apple, or a giant sledge hammer (okay, we just threw that last one in for fun). Get creative and think about how a simple prop can attract the attention of the audience, help you make your point, and communicate your message more effectively.

Cynthia Oelkers using a penny as a prop for her presentation
http://www.CorporateOvations.com/cynthiaprop

Whiteboard

In 2007, UPS (United Parcel Service) launched a campaign of commercials with a man standing in front of a whiteboard drawing pictures to tell a story of UPS logistics success. As he was drawing and telling the story, he was using a brown (UPS corporate color) marker. These commercials were amazingly simple and wildly successful. Audiences were mesmerized by the quick simple drawings that told the UPS story.

UPS Whiteboard Commercial
http://www.CorporateOvations.com/upswhiteboard

You don't have to be a skilled artist to successfully use a whiteboard; you just need to be sincere. In a prospective customer's office if you are selling your services and the prospect asks, "What makes you guys different from every other service provider out there?" You might have a slick brochure from your marketing department explaining the three key areas of your expertise and how you are the only provider in the region that can provide all three of those services.

But, you could also ask if you could use the whiteboard in their office. Then, draw a Venn diagram of three overlapping circles of services. You write the names of a few well-known brands in one or two of the circles and then you write your company name in the intersection of all three circles. You show that your company is the only provider that can deliver services in all three areas. Which would be more effective or impactful with your audience? Sometimes a simple whiteboard can be a powerful visual aid.

Flip Charts

If you are presenting in a training room or a conference room, you may have a large flip chart of paper sheets available. The flip chart has similar benefits to the whiteboard with one key difference; the flip chart sheets can be saved for later use by tearing them off and hanging them on the wall. If you choose to use a flip chart for a visual aid, plan what you will write and where you will stand. We've seen presenters spend too much time writing (creating an awkward silence in the room), and blocking the visual from the audience by where they stand.

Flip charts can create a dynamic participation by providing sheets to attendees and allowing them to write on the sheets. The sheets can be hung around the room and reviewed by you and the group.

You as the Visual

You can be a visual aid for the audience. In Chapter 9, you learned about the communication you send through body language. To be a visual aid, you could act out an example. In our workshops we act out the role of the speaker by delivering an opening to a presentation using an improvisational style. We ask the audience for a typical presentation situation they experience at work. Then we ask for a purpose and a description of the target audience. Finally, using the audience's information, we create an opening to a fictitious presentation on the spot and immediately deliver it to the workshop students.

We could have shown pre-recorded videos of actors delivering several types of openings based on different presentation scenarios. But by choosing to demonstrate the opening, we're able to personalize the example based on the suggestions from our audience.

Videos

This method is getting much easier to facilitate because of technology. Today most people carry a video camera in their pocket courtesy of their smart phone. If a senior executive cannot attend your meeting (much like an actor unable to attend the awards ceremony to receive an award), a pre-recorded message from the senior executive can be played for the group. With technology today, live streaming video can also be implemented. For example, you can have the senior executive join the presentation for a few minutes live via videoconference from another location.

In our workshops we use recorded videos of professional speakers delivering keynotes and presentations as examples of how to implement what we teach. If you are going to use a video as a visual aid, the audience appreciates it if you set up and debrief the video so they gain a full appreciation for why you included it in the presentation.

For videos you find online, always make sure you adhere to copyright laws and gain permission (depending on usage terms, you could be in violation of ethical codes of conduct or copyright laws). You are welcome to use any of our YouTube videos in your presentations (we simply ask that you give us credit).[8]

Don't underestimate the power of a simple overhead projector and a marker.

Old-School Overhead Projector with Transparencies

Seriously? You bet. One of the most profound presentations we have seen took place in the Marquee Ballroom at the MGM Grand Hotel in Las Vegas in front of an audience of 5,000. You could have heard a pin drop when the lights went out and a single center stage spotlight illuminated an old-school overhead projector next to an empty stool.

A 30-something man walked out onto the stage dressed to look intelligent, but unassuming. He was an ideal candidate for a professor at your local junior college. Without a word he turned on the overhead lamp and uncapped a marker to begin drawing. He began to speak as he drew a diagram of the Internet (the cloud) and the round trip all data packets take to move from the user to the Internet, to the data center and then back to the user.

The speaker had a simple purpose. Explain the complex services offered in a simple manner so all the sales professionals fully understand what makes us different. It was a simple explanation and it was extremely memorable. In a more profound way, the intersection of old-school technology and new-age services created an atmosphere with no intimidation. The services may be complex, but they can be explained with something as simple as an overhead projector and a marker. The irony of using old technology to explain the simplicity of the complex new technology was both appreciated and extremely effective.

Handouts

In some cases, corporate business presentations can be more effective if the attendees have a handout in front of them. Handouts are extremely useful when you will be reviewing complex diagrams with small print or detailed financials. If you show a slide on the projection screen for these kinds of detailed elements, the audience might not be able to see all the information. When the first words out of your mouth are, "I know you can't read this but ..." our question to you is, "If we can't read it then why did you include it?" Everyone deserves to have a front row seat. Print the diagram or slide as a handout and provide it to the attendees before you begin.

That last sentence may have just conjured up a question in your mind, "What is the rule on giving the handouts before, during, or after the presentation?" We are not big on rigid rules for presenting and communicating, because you can always find an exception. However, here is a general rule we use for handouts. If the presentation is full of information, details, charts, facts, and numbers then it is best to distribute your handouts in advance so the audience can more easily follow and refer back to any data they need during the presentation. If the handouts contain information that can detract from the impact of the presentation (a spoiler) or if the handouts are only needed as reference for later, you can hold them until after the presentation. Otherwise, they will simply be a distraction while you are presenting.

Don't fall into the trap of thinking you should use a print out of your slides as your handout. Your projected slides and your handouts do not have to match. Many speakers get lazy with their handouts and simply put all the information on the slides, then print the slides for the audience. When speakers do this, they risk overcrowding their slides and increase the chance that they'll just read the slides during their presentation (or worse—their audience will read them and not listen to the speaker).

An easier solution for differentiating your slides from the handouts is to use the *Speaker Notes* option in Microsoft PowerPoint®. When editing your slideshow, the text window below the slide is used for entering your speaker notes. By design, this is meant for the presenter to document their notes to be used when speaking.

Instead of using this section for the speaker notes, you can enter all the notes you want to provide to your audience in a handout. Then, instead of printing just the *slides* for your audience, you can print the speaker notes (located in the PowerPoint® Print Dialog box). Now you can distribute these handouts to the audience, and they will have a picture of the simple slide at the top, and all the detailed notes at the bottom.

Designing and Interacting with Your Slides

Since video projected slides are so prevalent in today's corporate environment, we cannot write a chapter on visual aids without giving them special attention. In this section, we will review methods for creating powerful slides, interacting with the slides, and delivering the slides professionally.

Don't commit a presentation
homicide when you present.

Designing Slides

Never forget that the *slides* are meant to support *you*, not the other way around! If you need a slide to support your subject, create one. If you don't need a visual slide to support a point you want to make, don't use one. This is a difficult concept for attendees in our workshops to grasp because we have all been over exposed to corporate presentations where slides are expected.

Often in these "presentations gone wrong," each slide contains nothing but bullet point after bullet point with an overabundance of text. Read this carefully: you do not need a slide for everything you say in a presentation! Don't fall into the trap of committing presentation homicide when you present (i.e., bullet point after bullet point with an overabundance of text).

> "Simplicity is the
> ultimate sophistication."
> **—Leonardo da Vinci,**
> Artist, Scientist, Inventor, and Writer

Have you ever looked at a *Where's Waldo?* book?[9] They're great fun for young children (and some adults!) because there is no reading involved, just pictures. Each turn of the page opens up into a two-page illustration of a scene with hundreds and hundreds of characters standing around in crowds, all doing something different. Wearing his traditional red and white striped shirt and stocking cap, Waldo is hidden somewhere on the two-page scene.

The object of the game is to play with someone else and see who can find Waldo first. As simple as it sounds, anyone who has played knows it can be quite difficult at times. When you overload your slides with words or pictures or diagrams, it can become quite difficult for your audience to pull out the most important point of the slide. Your message (your Waldo) gets lost in the clutter of your slide.

Less is more when it comes to designing slides.

Slides are visual aids, yet in presentations, we rarely see graphics or images used on any of them. Often, they just show text. There is nothing wrong with using bulleted text on a slide, but remember your audience has a very powerful visual learning modality.[10]

As an example, one of our workshop attendees was going to speak about how her company's customer service was superior to her competitors. She had four key points she wanted to talk about: her company's phone support, delivery services, web support and the awards her company had won. She created a slide with four bullet points, each containing a sub-bullet with detailed information on each of the four areas.

Customer Service Support

- **Phone Support**
  - We offer phone support 24 x 7 to answer all of your needs from the time you purchase to delivery
- **Free delivery**
  - In our delivery area we can deliver the product direct to your store, usually in the same day.
- **Web solutions and support**
  - If you have any questions, our web site has chat capabilities and a constantly updated FAQ page
- **Award winning service**
  - We have been awarded "Best Customer Service" Department by the American Business Awards 3 times.

Proprietary and Confidential

iSpeak

After our classroom discussion on using the *Six By Six Rule*, she decided to shorten her slide to only four bullet points with a couple key words for each of the four areas. Her slide looked much more concise than the overcrowded first version of the slide. Next, understanding that it is called a *visual* aid for a reason, she also decided to add a clip art graphic out to the side of the text.

Research documented in the Educational Communication and Technology Journal looked at 46 different experiments using combinations of text and graphics or text only to complete a task. In 45 out of the 46 experiments, the people with pictures along with text outperformed the text only participants.[11] By adding the simple graphic of a call center phone support woman, our workshop attendee enhanced the understanding of her message for her audience.

We challenged her to get creative and create one more version. We were quite proud when she came back to show us her updated slide. In the center was a picture of a woman representing the customer. The four corners around her were additional graphics, each depicting why her company provided exceptional customer service. The four graphics included a business desk phone, a screen shot of a support web site, a delivery truck, and the logos of three awards for customer service. All of the text had been removed in lieu of the graphics, making her message easier to interpret.

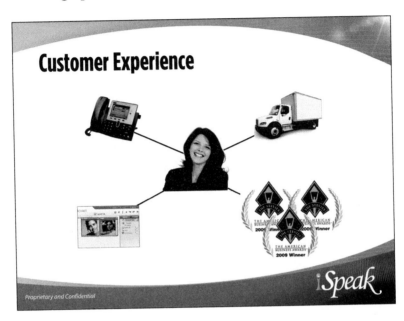

Be honest, as an audience member is it easier to read the description of her slide, or is it easier to just look at the pictures? Sometimes pictures can convey your message better than text alone and your audience will remain focused on you as the speaker.

> "Slides are slides. Documents are documents. . . .
> Attempts to merge them are called slideuments."
> —**Garr Reynolds,** Communications Expert and Author

Interacting with the Slides

In our years of delivering workshops to thousands of students, we have seen some interesting interactions with slides and projectors. In one workshop we had a rather portly gentleman walk up to the front of the video projector and stand directly in front of it, about 12 inches from the lens. This created a small projection of a blurry slide on his white-shirt. It actually looked like he had swallowed a small television. He told us later he was trying to block the projection because he wanted all eyes back on him. Mission accomplished! We guarantee everyone in that workshop was looking directly at him.

Another student had blacked out the screen with an actual black slide in her deck. Then, she had moved the mouse so the pointer was now the only image visible on the projected black screen. She was unaware of the mouse pointer image being projected on her screen. As she took a step forward closer to the actual projector the mouse pointer image was projected smack dab in the middle of her forehead. Every time she would step backward it would disappear, and then when she stepped forward it would sit right on her forehead again. This was a major distraction for the audience.

Another student interacting with his slides simply stood in the light of the projected image as he pointed to text on the screen. He became blinded by the dazzling light and had projected text and images across his chest and face. He actually looked like a chameleon as he took on the appearance of his slides.

These are all visual aid blunders that can distract from your message. When you deliver a presentation using slides, it is important to choreograph how you will interact with the projected image. If you plan on having slides with bulleted text, it is recommended that you position yourself to the left of your screen. As you gesture with a hand to the slide, the audience's eyes will follow down your arm and straight across the bulleted text. Because we read left to right, standing to the left will be comfortable for the audience as you gesture to the slides.

When you want your audience to focus on you, black out the screen. This allows the audience to feel as if they are interacting solely with you, which can build credibility and trust.[12] As you continue to present, all eyes from the audience will be brought back to the only thing moving and making sound in front of them—you.

Blacking out the screen can be done in both PowerPoint® and Keynote® using the *B-key* on the keyboard. Simply pressing *B* will black out the projected slideshow, while any key on the keyboard will toggle the slide back on to the screen. If you use a clicker to advance your slides, most have a blackout button available to you. The screen should be blacked out when a slide is not necessary and you want all attention back on you.

Of course, this is a balancing act because if you turn your slides on and off too often, it can become a distraction. Practice this technique and get feedback from members of your audience to gauge if it was too much, too little, or just right.

When you want all attention to come back to you, black out the screen using the B-key on the keyboard.

Effective Use of the Clicker

If you present on a regular basis, we highly recommend that you invest in a clicker to advance your slides.[13] If you are going to make the investment, there are several items in a wide range of prices to consider. Less expensive models will most likely be infrared remote controls. These work like your TV remotes at home and have to be pointed directly at the receiver to work. More expensive options use either Bluetooth or radio frequency control.

Although they're more expensive, we do recommend the latter. With a radio frequency control, the remote does not have to be pointed in line-of-site at the receiver to function properly, which will give you more freedom during your presentation.

Some other features to look for in a quality clicker are volume control for your laptop, a laser pointer and a digital timer with a countdown vibrate alarm. These other features are not required, but they can be extremely helpful when presenting. Use your budget to gauge which bells and whistles you want. If you prefer not to purchase a separate device and are good with your smartphone, applications are available that turn your smart devices into clickers.

When you use a clicker there is only one rule: do not allow the clicker to become a distraction for the audience. We recommend holding it at all times so you don't set it down and forget where it is. It should be held in your non-gesturing hand, or placed in your pants pocket. Do not shake it, slap it in your hand, tap it on a desk, or point it at people. We are not asking you to act like a magician palming the disappearing ball, but we don't ever want the clicker to distract the audience's from your message.

Pictures on a Slide as a Backdrop

As you saw in Chapter 7, stories can deliver a powerful punch to your presentation. If you are going to share a story in your presentation, you might consider using a picture on a slide to set the stage. For example, in a story about two people in a canoe used to illustrate teamwork, you could put a picture of a canoe docked at the shore behind you.

In our workshops, we share a story about sand dollars you find on the beach. The backdrop slide is a simple picture of a sand dollar. Much like a green screen used in movie production for placing the actor in just about any setting, you can set your own environment with pictures behind you while you tell your story.

One of the best speakers we've seen that effectively uses pictures as a backdrop is Steve Uzzell. Steve spoke at the 2010 Chick-fil-A Leadercast Conference and delivered a captivating presentation titled, "Open Roads Open Minds: An Exploration of Creative Problem Solving." Using only photographs as illustrations, Steve inspired the audience to learn from his journey and create their own adventures.[14]

Pecha Kucha

The *Pecha Kucha* (Japanese for chit-chat) method for presenting was first utilized in 2003 by Astrid Klein and Mark Dytham in Tokyo.[15] This style of presenting uses 20 slides with 20 seconds of speaking on each slide. If you do the math, you'll figure out that that means the total delivery time is limited to six minutes and forty seconds. This style keeps presentations fast paced and concise. Since 2003, Pecha Kucha Nights (PKNs) have been started in over 500 locations around the world. At these gatherings, speakers come prepared to deliver their message in the allotted 6 minutes and 40 seconds.

Depending on the purpose of your presentation and your audience, you can borrow from this style to create a fast-paced delivery that conveys your message in the most concise manner. Guy Kawasaki, former Apple fellow, uses this type of presentation style. He says your slides should complement your presentation, not dominate it.[16] Most of the presentations you see in this format use graphics much more than words on slides. The style has become quite popular and we speculate it will become even more mainstream in business as the millennial generation moves up in the corporate ranks of the business world. This generation is tuned into instant answers, faster results and more concise communication.

Prezi®, the Dynamic Presentation Canvas

Another presentation creation tool to rival PowerPoint® and Keynote® is a tool delivered to desktops through Software as a Service (SaaS) using cloud based computing. The tool touts itself as a dynamic presentation canvas that allows the audience to zoom through a presentation as if you were actually stepping into it.

Of course, the difficulty with all new tools is the novelty of the features. You may remember the first time you discovered how to fly in your bullets on the screen in PowerPoint®. You may have used that feature along with spins, sounds and flashing graphics, but eventually the novelty wore off and many of those features became distractions. Prezi®[17] offers amazing capabilities to tell a story in a fluid method instead of the linear process of creating a deck of slides. Our only caution to you is to be careful not to create distractions for your audience. It is important to keep their full attention on the message and the theme of your presentation.

You Have Choices

Just like Steven Spielberg has choices for the set, lighting, makeup and costumes in his productions, you have choices in choosing the visual aids for your presentations. As you complete the content for your presentation, you can start thinking about the types of visual aids that will help you captivate the audience and convey your message.

We challenge you to step outside the predictable deck of slides and use more of the tools you have available to you. As technology continues to change, we will all have more options to choose from. Always remember, visual aids should support you and your message. Don't let your visual aids become the presentation. *You* are the presentation.

CHAPTER HIGHLIGHTS

- To effectively inform and ultimately persuade your audience, simply telling the audience may be the least effective and least memorable method.

- Visual aids come in many forms:
  › A Prop
  › Whiteboard
  › Flip Charts
  › You as the visual
  › Videos
  › Old-school overhead projectors
  › Handouts
  › Video projected slides (PowerPoint® and Keynote®)

- You can make a great impact with a slide as a visual if you keep it simple—follow the *Six By Six Rule*; no more than six lines of six words for any slide.

- Sometimes pictures can convey your message better than text alone.

- Position yourself to the left of your screen. Because we read left to right, this is more comfortable for the audience as you gesture to the slides.

- Blacking out the screen can be done in both PowerPoint® and Keynote® using the *B-key* on the keyboard.

- Purchase a clicker to advance your slides to cut down on the distraction of moving to and from your laptop.

─────── **TOMORROW'S CHALLENGE** ───────

As you prepare for your next presentation, answer these questions:

☐ What visual aid mistakes have I seen or used in the past?

☐ Which types of visual aids could I use to effectively convey my message?

☐ How could I use visuals to capture my audience's attention and not distract from my core message?

CHAPTER 11

Handling Questions

*"I wish I had an answer to that
because I'm tired of answering that question."*

—Yogi Berra, Hall of Fame Catcher,
New York Yankees

The entire sales presentation given to the executive decision committee had been flawless up to this point. The sales rep could sense the timing was right and he wanted to hand the contract over for the approving signature. Before he did that, however, he asked, "Are there any questions?"

After an awkward silence the CEO spoke up, "Just one. The payback period final date on your last proposal was August 23rd. Why is the date now listed as September 9th in this proposal?"

The sales rep stands in silence as he looks around the room. Was it a cold chill or a bead of sweat he felt go down his neck? In the silence the VP of Operations sits back in his chair and crosses his arms as he waits. The Director of Marketing lowers her glasses and peers over the rims at the hesitant sales rep. What seems like a month of silence was actually only five seconds, but the feeling of gravity in the room is weighing down on the sales rep's shoulders as he contemplates what to say next. Not having a good response at the ready, he can feel the sale slipping away along with the audience's perceived confidence in him.

Have you been there before? A tough question gets lobbed at you from out of nowhere and all the credibility built over time vanishes in a matter of seconds. How you handle questions from the audience will do one of two things for the presenter. It will either help or hurt their credibility. Rarely does a question and answer session leave the perception of the speaker the same.

In sales, when the salesperson is cautious or reluctant when responding to a question, they risk losing credibility and trust with the customer.[1] But when handled effectively, the questions and answers can add to the speaker's credibility. This can be done if the speaker delivers strong responses and if the process for delivering the response is smooth.

"It is better to ask some of the questions than to know all the answers."[2]
—**James Thurber**, Cartoonist and Author

Expect the Tough Questions, Then Prepare

In Chapter 1 of this book, we discussed overcoming fear and anxiety associated with speaking. One of the most important methods for overcoming this fear is to be prepared for tough questions.

Because we are big fans of optimism it pains us a little to say this, but when it comes to taking questions from the audience, always prepare for the worst. Prepare for the worst, but expect the best! If you've analyzed your audience and how they feel about your topic, it shouldn't be too difficult to think up the tough questions they might ask you. Write those questions down and then brainstorm how you would respond to them if asked by an audience member.

For the extremely tough questions and high stakes speaking engagements you should role-play your responses with someone else to simulate the actual setting. In 1992, we were about to present to a manager of training and development at IBM. We documented all of the tough questions she might ask us. Then we took turns role-playing as the salesperson to work through our delivery of the response. Going into the presentation our nerves were already set on high-anxiety, but because we had rehearsed the answers to the tough questions, we were confident in our delivery.

When Should I Answer Questions?

When it comes to taking questions from the audience the speaker has several options. You can take questions throughout the presentation, hold all questions until the designated time, or not allow questions at all. The method you choose will depend on your purpose, the situation, and your audience. Think about what you are trying to achieve and think about whom you are addressing in the presentation.

If you allow questions to be asked throughout your presentation you gain the benefit of connecting with the audience at a conversational level. Most audience members will appreciate your willingness to answer their questions when they first pop up in their mind. The benefit in taking questions as they arise is that the attendees don't have to hold a question until later. It also allows the audience to guide the message and fill in missing information throughout the presentation.[3]

The downside to taking questions at any time is that you will be turning over control of the presentation to the audience more often than you may want. If questions are asked about upcoming topics you were going to cover, you will need to jump to that topic or tell the audience member to wait on that answer until you get further along in the presentation. If the presentation becomes too conversational, an audience member can potentially dominate the entire meeting and take the entire group down a different conversational path.

If you don't allow questions at all, you may drive a wedge between you and the audience because they will feel you are disconnected from them and their needs. In small settings, this will make the audience feel awkward. However, if you are delivering a keynote presentation on a stage to a large audience, it may be entirely acceptable and expected for you to preclude all questions.

If there is a series of speakers, the audience will appreciate you keeping the entire day on schedule by not taking questions. If you find yourself in this type of situation, but you still want to connect with the audience and take questions, offer your contact information before or after you speak so the audience members can contact you at a later time.

If you set a designated time for questions, you can maintain a tighter control on the entire presentation while still preserving a connection to the audience by responding to their specific interests and needs. The downside to taking questions at one designated time is that it will force attendees to remember their questions until that time. Even if they do remember to write down their question, by the time they ask it, they may point you back to something you said at the very beginning of your presentation. If you are using slides as visual aids, you will have to decide to jump around your slide deck or address it verbally and then continue with your presentation.

If you decide to designate a certain time for answering questions, we recommend that you not plan that time for the very end of your delivery. This is how most presentations in business are delivered today and it is unfortunate because speakers who do so set their entire presentation up to end on a possible poor question or poor response.

Instead of just taking questions at the end of your time slot, reserve the final couple of minutes for you to give the audience your closing remarks. This puts an exclamation point on your delivery because you can control the last word on your subject. With our suggestion to take questions just before your final remarks, you will take questions after the body of your presentation, but before you close. You can set this up by saying, "Are there any questions before I give you my closing remarks?" This will signal to the group that it is now question and answer time, but you also have a few words to say to wrap everything up.

> "There are no stupid questions;
> just obvious answers . . .
> or overlooked questions . . .
> or badly worded questions."[4]
> **—Daniella Kessler**, Poet and Author

When our students first hear our suggestion to take questions before the close of their presentations, it sounds awkward to them. Many of them say something like, "That's not how we do it here. We always take questions at the end."

Of course, we politely try and steer them in a different direction because we don't think you should take questions at the end. In fact, we are fairly certain everyone gives some kind of final remarks after the question and answer session. You wouldn't respond to the last question, stand up from the conference table, grab your belongings and walk out of the room in complete silence, right? Of course not!

You probably close after your final question and answer with something like, "Great. That's all I have today. Thank you all for coming. Please let me know if you have any questions later this week. Thanks." Even if the words are slightly different, we are willing to bet you say something after your last question, even if it is nothing more than "Thank you."

Put some thought into those final words. After you answer your last question, how are you going to wrap up the entire presentation? What will you say? The last thing you say might just be the first thing they recall after the presentation.

How Should You Respond to Questions?

"So when the question is asked, how should I respond?" The process for responding to questions, regardless of when they are asked is what we call "acknowledge, repeat, respond." The acknowledgment is nothing more than recognizing a person for asking a question. When you attend a presentation and an audience member asks a question, what is the first thing you usually hear the speaker say? "Great question!" This is their form of acknowledgment.

As much as we want to hear your acknowledgment, don't use this one. Don't get in a habit of grading the questions. When you start grading questions, the audience may now come to expect you will grade everyone's questions ... "Great question!" "Excellent question!" "Good question!" If you begin this practice and then someone asks a question and you don't grade it, how might that audience member feel? Is it possible they might think they have asked a less than satisfactory question since you didn't even grade it? Even if it is just a slight chance, there is still a possibility that someone may feel that way. As a speaker we should be doing everything we can to connect with audience members, not alienate them.

Rather than grading everyone's question, it is a good practice to just thank the participant for the question. In addition, you may choose to acknowledge them physically with your body language. Giving them eye contact, you could take a receiving pose (hands behind the back in handcuffs), or step toward the audience member and gesture with your palm open.

Once you acknowledge them for asking the question, step two is to repeat the question. When you repeat it, play it back to them with your interpretation. Don't be an audio recorder and play back the exact same words they said. Repeat it back with meaning. You could even preface your response with a comment like, "Let me make sure I have this correct. You are asking . . ." This will help you make sure you are answering the right question. After all, it is possible to hear the question, but misinterpret what the asker really wants to know. If that happens, you may end up providing the correct answer to the wrong question.

As you repeat the question, deliver the repeat of the question to the entire audience. This allows everyone to hear the question that was asked. In large audience venues when you are using a microphone to project your voice, repeating the question becomes a necessary courtesy to the entire audience so they can hear the question as well as your response.

Some will claim that the repeat of the question also gives you a few extra seconds to prepare your response. While that may be true, we hope there is no need to take a few extra seconds to think because we know you have already prepared for the tough questions!

The final step of the process is to respond. Since you repeated the question for the entire audience, you should deliver the response to the entire audience. So as you begin speaking, make eye contact and turn your body around the room to offer the response to everyone. While you can share the answer with the entire audience, it is just common courtesy to finish your response by acknowledging the person who asked the question.

When done with their response, some speakers will acknowledge that person again by either saying, "Thank you for the question." or "Does that answer your question?" Either form of closing acknowledgment is appropriate and the choice is left to the speaker.

What If You Don't Know the Answer?

In many cases, this is one of the main causes of fear and anxiety in speakers. The fear of getting a tough question and not knowing the answer plagues the minds of many presenters, but it doesn't have to be that way. When someone in your audience asks you a question, what do they want? This isn't a trick question, we promise. Just think about it. What do they want? That's right! They want an answer. When do they want it? Most people will immediately respond, "Ummm, now! That's why I asked you now!"

And that may be true. They'd like to have the answer now, but when do they really *need* the answer? If you don't know the answer to one of their questions, can you find that answer? Our guess is "yes" you can find that answer. You can find the answer and get it to her later.

> "I don't pretend to have all the answers.
> I don't pretend to even know
> what the questions are.
> Hey, where am I?"[5]
> —**Jack Handey**, Humorist and Author

When someone asks you a question and you don't know the answer, you need to get it for her. And, you need to set the expectation on when you will have it for her. When she asks the question and you are stumped, your response could be, "Thank you for the question. I don't have that information with me. Let me make a note. Can I get you a response by close of business tomorrow?"

Do you see how the first step is to admit you don't have the information? Stating your response this way instead of saying, "I don't know" sounds better because it doesn't insinuate anything about your knowledge level or IQ. Remember that speaking is not a smarts contest—no one is expected to know everything. If you don't know the answer, don't give bad information, and don't fake it.[6] Just write the question down and negotiate *when* you will get the response to her. If close of business tomorrow is unacceptable to her, she will let you know and change the expectation to something earlier, like close of business today.

Another option for you instead of just making a note and getting the answer for her is that you can assign the to-do item to the audience member. It would sound like this, "Thank you for the question. I don't have that information with me. Would you please make a note to send me an email with that request? I will research it for you and get a response to you within a day of receiving your email."

In this option for a response, the to-do item has been assigned to the audience member instead of the speaker. Based on the situation you can decide which response is most appropriate. One obvious determinant is based on who is asking the question and how they relate to you. Obviously, if your CEO is asking you the question, we don't recommend assigning that to-do item to her!

"No question is so difficult to answer
as that which the answer is obvious."[7]
—**George Bernard Shaw**, Irish Playwright

What If There Are No Questions?

If there are no questions during a designated question and answer time, you have a couple of options. You could simply move on to your close and wrap up the presentation or you could ask yourself a question. Just remember it is important to pause an appropriate amount of time before moving on to the close.

A quick side note, you should be curious about why there were no questions. The optimistic view is that you did a fantastic job presenting and because of that, there were no questions. Everyone completely understood everything! The pessimistic view is that the audience was not fond of you or your topic and they were just trying to get to the finish line.

If you are in sales and the prospective customer has no questions, it should be a concern. They may not be able to picture themselves using your product or service, or they have already decided not to purchase. If you are curious about the audience's lack of questions after you end your presentation, try to have a one-on-one conversation with an audience member to get their reaction to your presentation.

As we touched on above, the other response option when you don't receive any questions from the audience is to ask yourself a question. You could begin by saying, "One question I get asked quite often is ... " Several benefits can come from using this method. The first benefit is you get to ask yourself a question to which you have a great answer. When you ask a tough but fair question and knock it out of the park, you add to your credibility. The second benefit from asking yourself a question is that no one in the audience has to volunteer to ask a question first. The third benefit is that while you are answering your own question, it will give additional time for the audience to think of their own questions.

Your Credibility is on the Line

The question and answer time of any presentation can make or break the speaker's credibility. When you are prepared with responses and armed with the process of *acknowledge, repeat, respond*, the odds are in your favor to increase your credibility.

—————— **CHAPTER HIGHLIGHTS** ——————

- The question and answer section of a presentation, when handled effectively, can add to the speaker's credibility.

- When it comes to questions the audience may ask, prepare for the worst. Write down the tough questions they might ask you and then come up with your responses.

- If you designate a specific time for answering questions, we recommend you take questions after the body of your presentation, but before your closing remarks.

- The process for responding to questions, regardless of when an audience member asks the question, is:
  › Acknowledge
  › Repeat
  › Respond

- When someone asks you a question and you don't know the answer, don't fake it. Admit you don't have the information and get back in touch with the participant at a later time.

- If there are no questions during a designated question and answer time, you can share questions you've been asked on the topic, or proceed to your prepared close.

―――――― **TOMORROW'S CHALLENGE** ――――――

As you prepare for your next presentation, answer these questions:

☐ What are the tough questions your audience members might ask?

☐ When do you plan to address questions in your next presentation?

☐ How will you handle the situation when participants have no questions?

CHAPTER 12

Rehearsal and Evaluation

"Stop acting as if life is a rehearsal.
Live this day as if it were your last.
The past is over and gone.
The future is not guaranteed."

—Wayne Dyer,
Motivational Speaker and Author

The director of new product development was finishing his steak when the account manager said, "When we're done with dinner, let's step out into the lobby and we can review the presentation you'll be giving tomorrow to our customer." The director lowered his fork and knife and shot back, "Listen, I've been doing this a long time and I've given this presentation before. We'll be fine. I'm just going to wing it."

It doesn't take a super sleuth to figure out what happened the next day at the customer presentation. The senior executive from the corporate customer not only had trouble staying awake, but he actually stood up and walked out of the presentation 15 minutes before it was scheduled to finish.

After the meeting the account manager pulled a different customer VP aside to ask him privately for his thoughts on the meeting. "So how do you think that went?" he asked. With a frown on his face and glaring eyes, the customer VP replied, "I think you know." This example is based on a true story, and unfortunately, it's most likely not an isolated incident. Similar presentations-gone-wrong play out in front of potential customers and other disappointed audiences around the world every day.

Just because you know the content of a presentation does not guarantee that you'll nail the delivery in front of your audience. Just because you have no fear of speaking in front of others does not mean you are a great presenter. As you learned in Chapters 2 and 3, when the purpose of the presentation or the audience changes, but the presentation does not, it can lead to very different results.

"Wing it." Those two words get used often as if they are courageous and daring, when in fact they are nothing more than rude and arrogant. When "winging it" becomes the preparation process of choice (or lack thereof!), the people using it make the excuse that they are just too busy to rehearse and besides, they reason, they know this material better than anyone else! That's why they've been asked to speak! Rehearsal is not always about studying to understand the content better or to get over your stage fright. Rehearsal is the planning and preparation to successfully deliver the content to the audience.

Rehearsal increases your chances of
connecting with the audience.

In 1875, sculptor Frederic Auguste Bartholdi was commissioned to create Liberty Enlightening the World, better known today as the Statue of Liberty. He was an accomplished and respected sculptor in France. Ten years later when it came time to transfer the Statue of Liberty to the United States, he needed the assistance of Gabriel Lespinasse de Saulne, the Captain of the French frigate the Isere. Captain de Saulne would captain the ship that would ultimately deliver Lady Liberty to her permanent home on Bedloe's Island in New York Harbor.[1] While Bartholdi may have known everything about the statue and the sculpture, he did not pretend to know anything about piloting a vessel across the Atlantic or docking it at its port.

The moral of this story? Knowing a subject does not make you an expert in transferring that content to others. Your rehearsal is the practice of the *transfer* of your content.

Rehearsal is Not the Same as Practice

To rehearse effectively, we need to have a deep understanding of what we are trying to accomplish. It is also helpful to have a process or a series of steps to follow. To some, rehearsal means you take a few minutes to toss around some ideas in your head, think about your key points, and then prepare for the questions you might get at the end.

That is not rehearsal; that is practice. There is a big difference. If you've ever been in any kind of theatrical production, you are probably familiar with the phrase "let's run lines." When a group of actors wants to get comfortable with a scene, they will sit around a large conference table with their scripts while they read through the scene, each reading their own lines. This is practice for acting. When you do a quick review of your content, you are practicing.

If you've been in a theatrical production, you are also familiar with the term "dress rehearsal." And as you know dress rehearsals take place on the stage. Actors are in full costume. They are expected to have their lines memorized. In a dress rehearsal, actors will run through the scenes as if they are delivering them in front of a live audience. This form of rehearsal is very different from the practice of running lines.

Good directors will mandate as many run-throughs and dress rehearsals as possible prior to their first public appearance because they understand the importance of preparation.[2] In much the same way, your preparation for a corporate presentation should be practiced and rehearsed. Always rehearse standing up. Go through the movements you plan to use the day of the presentation and if possible, rehearse in the actual venue.

"There are always three speeches
for every one you actually gave:
The one you practiced, the one you gave,
and the one you wish you gave."
—**Dale Carnegie,** Speaker, Teacher, and Author of
The Quick and Easy Way to Effective Speaking

The Rehearsal Process

Often we get resistance from our workshop attendees about rehearsing because they worry it will take up too much of their time. We've heard, "I'm giving a one-hour presentation on this topic. I don't have extra hours in my day to rehearse this several times. Even if I don't want to wing it, I *have to*!"

Understanding that we have more requests to present in business than we do hours for rehearsal, we can still rehearse the most important elements of our delivery. As you learned in Chapters 4 and 5, the open and the close of your presentation are the bookends of your delivery. The first and last thing you say just might be the most remembered part of your presentation.

Because the open and the close are so important to your success, it's essential that you always rehearse them both. We often hear students in our workshops say, "I'm usually a little nervous and shaky at the start, but once I get going, I'm fine." This holds true for so many business presenters too. What better reason to spend some focused rehearsal time on your opening! In addition to the open and close, you should also select the critical elements from the body content and rehearse those pieces.

The first and last thing you say just might be the most remembered part of your presentation.

Rehearsal can be accomplished in a short period of time when you have a process to follow. The rehearsal process we teach includes three key steps after you have constructed your presentation and your visual aids:

1. Read the presentation out loud (open, close, key body elements)
2. Stand and deliver the presentation with your notes
3. Stand and deliver with no notes

The rehearsal process should be repeated several times with adjustments or corrections made each time. How much of the presentation you read and deliver and how many times you repeat it will be dependent on the length of the presentation and how much time you have to rehearse.

"It is the nature of man to rise to greatness if greatness is expected of him."
—**John Steinbeck,** Pulitzer Prize-winning Author of *The Grapes of Wrath, East of Eden,* and *Of Mice and Men*

Rehearsal Requires a Critic

When you think about actors rehearsing for a play, who sits out in the empty seats of the theater watching, listening and providing feedback? That's right . . . the director. Even if the actors practiced their lines and rehearsed on stage, if they never received any feedback prior to opening night, their delivery could fall flat with the audience. In a corporate environment, we need to seek feedback on our delivery so we can consistently improve.

Throughout his book *Outliers: The Story of Success*, Malcolm Gladwell claims that the key to success in any field is practice and feedback. He says that to a large extent, practicing a specific task for a total of around 10,000 hours and receiving feedback on our performance helps us continually improve.[3]

This feedback will come from three sources:

- You
- Your peers
- Your mentor or coach

You Are Your Best Critic

Speaking from experience, no one will be tougher on your performance than you. This is the reason why we give you two other sources for gathering feedback. The best part about using yourself as a critic is that you have total control over that critic's schedule! You can schedule time with you without much trouble.

The next question we are usually asked is, "How do I critique myself? Let me guess . . . present in front of a mirror!" Our response would be, "Actually, no. Don't do that." This tip is the first to come to mind because it has been around for decades. Many teachers taught their students to present in front of a mirror so they could see their delivery as the audience would see it. Then, they could critique themselves.

But when you speak in front of a mirror, you are truly multitasking. You are asking your brain to be the best presenter it can be while at the same time, be the toughest critic it can be. And you expect your brain to do all of this at the same time. You cannot expect to be the best at anything when you are doing two things at once.

Research in neuroscience has proven that multitasking actually makes the brain less efficient than single tasking your time[4]. Practicing in front a mirror was used for decades because it was the best method at the time. But with today's technology, that is no longer the case. Now, you probably have both an audio and a video recorder in your pocket courtesy of your smartphone. As Apple, Inc., says, "There's an app for that."[5]

If you want to critique yourself on video, hand your recording device to a friend and ask your friend to record you as you speak. If you want to work on your vocal delivery (eliminating filler words, slowing your pace, changing vocabulary, etc.), you can set your recording device on the lectern or the conference table and start the audio recorder app before you begin speaking.

When asked to deliver a custom keynote message, we will often times audio record our delivery several times, pick our best delivery, then transfer it to an iPod® so we can listen to it while flying to our destination. After you listen to your message, listen to it again. You will discover new critiques during a second listening that had escaped your attention the first time.[6] In today's technological world, it is much easier to critique your own delivery, but you shouldn't stop there.

Seek Feedback from Your Peers

Flixster® is a helpful application available for smartphone devices. It is a movie application, which shows you the movies currently playing in theaters as well as upcoming releases. One helpful feature is the ratings feature. For every movie currently showing it provides the percentage of critics and the percentage of users (people like you and me) who rated the movie with a simple thumbs up or thumbs down. Since we don't always agree with the ratings from professional film critics, it is nice to see the ratings of our peers.

Similarly, peer feedback is important when you're preparing for and/or trying to improve a presentation. Even if your friends have not taken a workshop on presentation skills, they can surely offer a simple thumbs up or thumbs down on your performance. Peer feedback will be most helpful if someone is willing and able to see you speak in person prior to the presentation. The key for most will be finding the time to make that happen.

If that isn't possible, don't forget about your ability to record audio and video with a smart device. If face-to-face peer review is not possible, audio or video recordings shared through email, Facebook® or YouTube® can be the next best thing. Even when one of us is in Singapore and the other is in Romania, we are still able to use tools like Skype® to provide each other with feedback on our upcoming presentation. With technology today the world is truly a much smaller place, but as Steven Wright[7] says, "I wouldn't want to paint it."

In a corporate setting, you will usually know a few members of your audience. After a presentation, ask them what they thought of your delivery. Selecting a peer friend who will be honest is critical. You do not want someone who responds with, "It was great. Good job." That doesn't help. Make sure that you always ask follow-up questions like, "What did you like/dislike about it?" and "What could I change for next time?"

One of the best people to recruit will be someone who also has an interest in improving their own presentation skills. That way you'll both have an accountability partner. You know how it is always easier to jog or get to the gym when you know you have someone else relying on you, the same goes for improving your speaking skills.

"Evaluate what you want—
because what gets measured gets produced."
—**James A. Belasco,** Speaker, Consultant, and Author

Find a Mentor or Coach

The best method for improving your presentation skills is to find a mentor or a coach who will be dedicated to your consistent improvement. A mentor is someone who possesses the skills you want to emulate. It could be a colleague, a friend, or someone outside your profession. Most mentors won't ask to be paid for the help they give you. They want to do it because they have a sincere interest in seeing you succeed. In some cases, the mentor simply sees a bit of herself in you and wants to help you avoid the mistakes she made along the way.

If you know of someone you could approach, keep in mind the mentor will most likely be flattered and at the same time fearful of the time investment. From the very start, it is in your best interest to communicate the expectations on time commitments. Proper mentoring can be done in as little as 15–30 minutes per week. It can be done over the phone or over lunch. Mentor relationships develop over time so be prepared to continue conversations for at least six months before reevaluating.

A coach, however, is often a paid position. If you want serious dedicated assistance, you can hire a professional speaking coach. Many of these individuals have obtained licensed certifications in professional coaching and many have their own development programs they bring with them. They will provide structure to the coaching conversations and the process for improvement.

Coaches, like mentors, are accountability partners for you. The speaking coach will have a wealth of knowledge to share and tools to help teach and train you. They may not have the same presentation style as you, but they have the know-how to raise your level of performance. Think of it like this. Even Tiger Woods has had different golf coaches work with him over the years.[8] Tiger is one of the best golfers of all time and his coaches cannot come close to achieving what he has accomplished on the golf course, and yet he still seeks their feedback on his golf game. He understands these coaches know the game, and they can tell him what he needs to do to improve his game. Speaking coaches are skilled and trained in the ways of speaking and presenting. They are experts at dissecting your performance and providing suggestions for improvement.

There is no best; there's always a better.

Always Seek to Improve

Whether you evaluate your own performance or seek feedback from others, no one will improve their performance without consistent evaluation, reflection and implementation of new skills.[9] A great presenter understands that there is no such thing as a best speaker, because there's always room to get *better*. Make rehearsal and evaluations a standard part of your speaking process. Don't just "wing it" ever again!

——————— **CHAPTER HIGHLIGHTS** ———————

- Many people make the excuse that they don't have time to rehearse so they decide to just "wing it." But the reality is rehearsal is an essential step in your presentation preparation and can be accomplished in a short period of time when you have a process to follow. The rehearsal process includes three key steps after you have constructed your presentation and your visual aids:
  - › Read the presentation out loud
  - › Stand and deliver the presentation with your notes
  - › Stand and deliver with no notes

- You need to seek feedback on the delivery of your presentation so you can consistently improve. This feedback can be done by yourself, can be provided by your peers, or can be delivered by a mentor or coach.

- Whether you evaluate your own performance or seek feedback from others, no one can improve their presentation skills without consistent reflection and continuous implementation of new skills.

——————— **TOMORROW'S CHALLENGE** ———————

As you prepare for your next presentation, answer these questions:

☐ What is your motivation to practice and rehearse?

☐ Which of the evaluation methods will you use for critique and feedback?

☐ Who will be your coach or mentor?

Implement to Improve

"You are only an attitude away from success."
—John C. Maxwell, Leadership Expert,
Speaker, Coach, and Author

You've made it to the end of the book. Unfortunately, if all you did was read it and place it on your bookshelf, then you just wasted your time. You probably didn't like the sound of that, but it's true. To really reap the benefits of what's in this book, you have to implement what you've learned. The information in this book was not meant to be only read, but also processed, understood, and applied.

Perfection is a direction, not a destination.

One thing we've learned over the years is that the more we learn, the more we learn that there is more to learn. In other words, if you want to remain at the top of your profession, there is no graduation date in life. As we've noted, Malcolm Gladwell[1] states that the prerequisite for great achievement is 10,000 hours of deliberate practice before you can really master a subject area or skill. In order to grow, you must acquire new or updated information and apply it directly to your situation on a consistent basis.

Our hope is that we have provided that information for you in *Corporate Ovations* and that you are inspired to want to make a change in your presentation and communication skills. But now comes the hard part—making a change.

Simply put, the world is divided into three categories: 1) those who can easily change—and do, 2) those who want to change—but get stuck, and 3) those who resist change—and never change.[2] We hope you're not in the final group, but then again, you probably wouldn't have read this book if you are!

If you are in the first group—good luck. And if you are in the middle group, like so many of us, our intent was to provide you with the techniques from our own experiences to help you get "unstuck." When you implement these techniques to improve your public speaking skills, your presentations at work will result in standing ovations—thus the name *Corporate Ovations!*

Everything is difficult, until it isn't.

Commit to Change

Any time we attempt something new or different, it starts out difficult until we get more comfortable and confident. Over time these new skills are no longer difficult. In fact, they can become quite enjoyable when we have mastered the craft. Think about when you first learned the alphabet, drove a car, or presented to an audience. At first your new responsibility was challenging, but the more you practiced, the more you improved, and the more you improved, the more you enjoyed the experience.

"Practice does not make perfect.
Only perfect practice makes perfect."
—Vince Lombardi,
Hall of Fame Football Coach, Green Bay Packers

In the introduction of this book we introduced you to a Japanese term called *Satori*. Hopefully you've recorded many "a-ha" or "light-bulb" moments as you've read the book, but now comes the hard part. Remember, nothing improves until something changes.

A new Japanese term we would like you to remember is *kaizen*—a word that refers to a philosophy of continuous improvement. "Kai" means change and "Zen" means good. The term *kaizen* translated at its fullest means "the willingness to constantly pursue improvement one small step at a time."

The only way to improve is to implement your new knowledge. This can be done in the form of a promise to take action on what you have learned. For example, you could commit to delivering a 9-minute presentation at an upcoming meeting.

Remember, focus on only one or two commitments at a time, because trying to implement too many changes at once can be overwhelming, decrease your efficiency, and ultimately create anxiety. We find it helpful to share our current goals and commitments with each other, so we can help, guide, and facilitate each other's plans. We strongly recommend finding a trusted friend or mentor who demands accountability—someone to help encourage you to completion.

> "Create a definite plan for carrying out your desire and begin at once, whether you are ready or not, to put this plan into action."
> —**Napoleon Hill,** Author of *Think and Grow Rich* and *The Law of Success*

21-day Challenge

Making commitments and forming new habits is hard work. Changing any habit takes practice—framing, forming, and molding our minds to adopt new behaviors means they must be repeated over and over again.

As you begin to implement what you have learned from this book, the new techniques may feel a bit forced, but as you practice the new skill over and over, it becomes a habit. Once it becomes a habit, it is no longer an effort.

The 21-day phenomenon is a concept that was developed by Dr. Maxwell Maltz, author of *Psycho-Cybernetics*.[3] Dr. Maltz discovered that you must persist in performing a new behavior for at least 21 days before a new behavior becomes automatic. After 21 days, it becomes easier. It becomes natural. It becomes a habit.

> "Ability is what you're capable of doing. Motivation determines what you do. Attitude determines how well you do it."
> —**Lou Holtz,** Hall of Fame College Football Coach, Sportscaster, Motivational Speaker, and Author

Corporate Ovations in Action

One of our customers and dear friends, Don Forrester, Vice President for Programs and Services for Children At Heart Ministries,[4] has attended several of our workshops. He is constantly looking for his next *Satori* so he can make a *kaizen* commitment.

Don does an outstanding job of communicating his message with the focus placed on his audience. It's clear that he constantly asks himself, *What does my audience want? What is my audience expecting?* Don told us he consistently uses our techniques in his presentations. We asked him if he would summarize some of his thoughts. This is what Don had to say about how these skills have positively affected him personally and at work.

Nothing is more satisfying than a good book. Consequently, I stop by the bookstore on a regular basis. Perhaps I am old fashioned, but I much prefer a hardback book to an electronic file. Somehow a bound copy makes the book seem more substantive and less temporary. Of course, my favorite books are those I can't put down after reading the first three pages. It doesn't happen often, but if I'm totally captivated after only turning a page or two, the chances are good that I will carve out the time to read the book non-stop.

I've attended several public speaking training sessions with Russ Peterson and Kevin Karschnik and a key principle they teach is also underscored here in *Corporate Ovations.* It is the absolute importance of opening with power. Your opportunity to captivate your audience can be won or lost in the first few seconds of your presentation. The impact and dynamic quality of the first words communicated to your audience are as critically important as the first three pages of a book. If you want your audience to be engaged in what you have to share, your window of opportunity to draw them in is fairly narrow. It begins when you start your presentation.

Consequently, I now understand the importance of crafting my words carefully and attempting to gain the audiences' undivided attention at the very beginning. It isn't simply that it is important to me professionally to be regarded as an effective communicator; it has more to do with my desire to honor the time of those in attendance by providing something substantive and thought provoking. I never stand before any group to speak in any capacity, even if it is simply introducing another speaker, without challenging myself to make my comments interesting and captivating.

As an example of what I'm talking about, I recently attended a Leadership Institute for a national organization for which I serve as a board member. Following the lunch break, the person coordinating the institute asked me if I had the information I needed to facilitate the next presentation. It was my responsibility to introduce three speakers comprising the next panel.

The very question pushed me into a sense of panic. I am sure my cortisol level rose immediately pushing me toward the "flight or fight" mode. I had no idea that the responsibility was mine. Talk about a failure to communicate. Someone had obviously dropped the ball.

I had the passing thought, "I'd rather have 'root canal' work than introduce three speakers that I know nothing about." How many boring minutes at every conference do we invest with someone sharing a presenter's biography only to subsequently hear them share it again in their presentation?

I quickly scanned the program for information I needed to introduce the panelists. It immediately became evident that my simply pronouncing each of their names correctly was going to be a challenge. There was no way in the few short minutes before the session that I could familiarize myself with the biographical details for me to feel comfortable sharing the information without reading it. I refused to do that. That is counter-productive to building a reputation that you are an effective communicator.

In the midst of an anxiety attack, I opted to draw from the toolbox of options provided to me through *Corporate Ovations*. I met each of the panelists before the meeting began and told them it was my privilege to introduce them to the conference participants. I asked if it was permissible to simply call the audiences' attention to the fact that biographical information was included in the program. They each agreed.

When I stood to speak, I simply said that it was my honor and pleasure to have the opportunity to welcome and introduce the next panelists. Miracle of miracles, I think I pronounced the names correctly. I referenced the fact that detailed information about each of the panelists was included in the program.

I moved on to say: "Although it is an honor for me to introduce today's panelists, I am perhaps the least qualified of anyone in attendance to be given that task. After gleaning information about them from the information included in the program, I recognized two things they each have in common. They each have analytical abilities and budgetary expertise. Don't both of those activities fall under the venue of 'left-brain' functioning? I thought so. I have no first-hand knowledge related to any of that. Left-brain functioning is not one of my strong suits. Truthfully, each member of the panel possesses synaptic connections that leave me a little envious. I am older than any of the panelists, but if they had been in elementary school when I attended, they would each have fallen in the 'blue bird reading group.' In short, all of their classmates would have regarded them as really, really, really smart! Please join me in welcoming . . ."

The introduction obviously worked. Even the panelists gave me applause and subsequently referenced the "blue bird reading group" several times throughout their presentations. One speaker said, "I really like that group designation."

My recent experience is simply one example of a public speaking crisis averted by simply taking the time to reflect on what I learned from *Corporate Ovations and opting to use the concept of opening with power.*

There are many venues in which I have opportunities to speak in public. Truthfully, I have discovered again and again that I intuitively go back to the principles Russ and Kevin have included in *Corporate Ovations.* I am not yet where I ultimately want to be, but I am on my way.

Final Thoughts

As we wrap up our journey through communication and presentation skills, we want you to keep something in mind. Success in business, and in life, begins with your commitment to continuous improvement with an expectation of accomplishment.[5] Commit to improvement and expect success. As you learn more about effective communication, the more you begin to realize the need to improve through the implementation of new skills, and that the only way you can truly improve is by constantly challenging yourself to implement new skills.

In our final thoughts for you, we have a word of caution and a word of encouragement. First, the word of caution: One thing you can count on for sure, the implementation of these new skills will be difficult. It will take a strong commitment on your part involving your head, your heart and your hands. Without the commitment to implementation, improvement will be impossible.

Next, the word of encouragement: It's worth every minute! While we may never reach perfection in our communication skills, we will never stop pursuing improvement for the sake of our audience. When you give the audience what they want, when your message has satisfied their needs, when you have truly connected with your audience, they will respond with genuine thanks and more than just hearty applause. They will respond with *Corporate Ovations!*

Acknowledgments

First and formost we give glory and thanks to God, who had a plan when he brought together two eleven-year-old boys in the front yard to play football, start businesses, and make a positive difference in the lives of those around them.

Jeremiah 29:11

This book is not just the work of two friends; it is the result of everyone who has been a part of our lives since we first met in 1979. Who knew the lemonade stand would turn into a lifetime of entrepreneurial ventures?

Thank you to our parents for believing in us even when they saw our entire college tuition walk away from Fortune 500 jobs to begin an entrepreneurial journey.

Kevin wants to thank his family for all their encouragement throughout the process of this project. We could not have written this book without a strong foundation at home.

Russ wants to thank his family for the understanding and support during all those late evenings on the computer in the home office. The love and encouragement was the fuel needed to complete this project. Thanks for believing in us.

Thank you to all of our corporate customers who have attended our training programs and workshops. Specifically, we want to thank Margie Poole, Toni Bailey Nottingham, Don Forrester, Reid Ryan, and Charley Ayres. We appreciate your business and we value your friendship.

We owe a tremendous amount of gratitude to all the talented and professional individuals we've had the pleasure to work with at iSpeak, specifically, Dara Kukla, Bill Kreiger, and Cynthia Oelkers.

Thank you to the thousands of students worldwide who over the years provided feedback that helped us improve our workshop content and methodology. Your stories of how our tools brought life-changing effects were more than we could have ever imagined. Thank you for allowing us to walk with you on a journey toward greater communication.

Special thanks to Barry Kerrigan and Del LeMond at Desktop Miracles for the editing, cover design, and publishing. Thanks for turning our vision into reality.

About the Authors

K evin Karschnik and Russ Peterson Jr. share a common passion for eradicating poor presentations from the landscape of business. Their careers have allowed them to speak to thousands of people around the world. Drawing from their experience while delivering keynote speeches, workshops and seminars, their process has been refined into the blueprint you hold in your hands now. All the best!

Kevin Karschnik is an author, speaker, and corporate trainer. He is co-founder of iSpeak, Inc. with Russ Peterson Jr., a company focused on helping people inform, inspire, implement, and improve. He uses humor and his broad business knowledge to present to audiences ranging from Corporate Executives to Sales Representatives to Leadership Teams. Kevin has presented to thousands of individuals across the United States and around the world, including companies such as CenterPoint Energy, The Houston Astros, AT&T, Dell, and The Ronald McDonald House. Kevin graduated from The University of North Texas and he lives in Round Rock, Texas, with his wife, two children, and a dog, Lily.

Russ Peterson Jr. co-founded FutureTech Training in 1991. After growing this business to three locations in Texas, he sold the company to an international competitor. After excelling in sales and business development with Fortune 500 companies like GTE and CSC, Russ co-founded iSpeak, Inc. (www.iSpeak.com) with Kevin Karschnik. iSpeak teaches effective communication with presentation skills through workshops, feedback and coaching for salespeople, leaders and individual contributors. As a trainer, professional speaker, and corporate representative, Russ has delivered keynotes and seminars for thousands of individuals around the world. His international audiences have been in places like Amsterdam, Ireland, Italy, Romania, Singapore, and Malaysia. Russ is also the author of *Cut the C.R.A.P. and Make the Sale* (DC Press, 2003). He lives in Round Rock, Texas, with his wife, two children, and a black lab.

"The class that Russ Peterson delivered was the most impressive training I have ever attended in my 17 years in telecom. I have recommended his workshop to several businesses and customer contacts."

—AARON VORWALD, XO Communications

"Kevin really knows his stuff—he was eloquent, diplomatic, professional, engaging, inspiring, and very astute to the dynamics of the class. I hope to one day be as good as him! Superior training!"

—GAIL WEBB, AMD

CORPORATE
OVATIONS

Now that you've read the book . . .
What's next?

Start a movement!

Join the thousands of others who have committed
to putting an end to boring presentations.

www.CorporateOvations.com

Connect

www.facebook.com/corporateovations www.youtube.com/corporateovations

www.twitter.com/CorpOvations   www.CorporateOvations.com

Tools

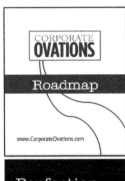

www.CorporateOvations.com

Bulk Orders

Corporate Ovations can be ordered in bulk. Whether you need 25 or 5,000 copies, we can help. Bulk orders are great for corporate gifts, sales conference breakout sessions, university business school special events or church leadership training. The Group Discussion Guide (PDF) available at CorporateOvations.com is a free tool designed to help small groups get the most out of the book. Discounts are available for quantities as small as 25 books. If you would like to place a bulk order, please contact us at info@CorporateOvations.com

Special Offer

Access the accompanying online video library for *Corporate Ovations* at iSpeak University. Use the Promo Code below to receive 50% off the registration and access to videos which parallel the *Corporate Ovations* book.

ww.iSpeak.com/ispeak-university
ISPEAKU50

Group Study

The *Corporate Ovations* Group Study kit is ideal for you to conduct your own mini-training sessions on the skills taught in the book. Let Russ and Kevin teach you their workshop through video lessons. Then facilitate your own interactive exercises to practice your new skills. Group sessions work best with up to 10 participants.

Facilitator Kit

- Facilitator Guide & Instructor training videos
- Video lessons for the workshop taught by Russ and Kevin
- Copy of the participant guide
- Audio version of the book *Corporate Ovations*

Participant Guides

- Participant guides for each attendee

Self-Study

The *Corporate Ovations* Self-Study kit is designed for individuals interested in further improving their personal communication skills with the techniques taught in *Corporate Ovations*. The Self-Study guide comes with:

- Video lessons taught by Russ and Kevin
- Participant workbook
- Audio version of the video lessons
- Audio version of the book *Corporate Ovations*

Speaking

Need a professional speaker who can inspire while developing new skills? Russ Peterson, Jr. and Kevin Karschnik will leave your audience informed, inspired, and ready to improve!

Corporate Ovations Keynote

It's not what you say that's important, it's what they hear! As speakers we all have a goal or purpose for speaking, but too often we forget that the audience is there because they have a goal or purpose for listening. When we place the focus of speaking where it needs to be (on the audience) we are able to construct the right message. In this keynote the authors share the three key areas of focus for effective presentations – Prepare for the right audience, develop effective visuals, and deliver an engaging and memorable message. Don't let your next presentation end in a sigh of relief from your audience. Learn how to end your presentation with a *Corporate Ovation*!

9-Minute Presentations Keynote

According to Opinion Matters research in 2012, 50% of time in meetings is wasted. Much of this can be attributed to poor presentations rambling aimlessly for far too long. We can cure this issue by starting a movement within our organizations to incorporate 9-Minute Presentations. If you have ever said to yourself after watching a presentation, "There was a whole lot that just wasn't necessary," then you need to know about this effective and timesaving method for presenting. While not every presentation can take on the 9-minute format, far too many 60-minute presentations can. In this keynote the authors share the research behind the selection of 9 minutes, as well as the template for how to construct and deliver this effective form of presentation. Learn how to improve the effectiveness of your meetings while saving time and money for your organization. Join the movement today!

Workshops

The ability to communicate ideas and influence others through public presentations is consistently ranked as a top quality sought by employers today. Become a polished and persuasive public speaker!

Corporate Ovations for Business Professionals (2 days)

Business professionals in management, HR, finance, or IT can benefit from this two-day workshop. All participants will learn the methods from the book and practice their skills with video recordings plus coaching and feedback.

Corporate Ovations for Sales Professionals (2 days)

Sales professionals present to some of the toughest audiences – prospective customers. Using methods from the book, attendees will learn to align their proposals to their audiences. Presentations will be video recorded and each participant will receive feedback and coaching.

Corporate Ovations for Leaders
(3 day workshop, plus 6 hours of private coaching)

Leaders and executives have unique needs for developing speaking skills because they tend to have the widest array of potential audiences from the Board of Directors, to the media, to their team of employees. In this workshop facilitated exclusively by the authors, participants will learn and practice the *Corporate Ovations* presentation methods. Attendees will also receive 6 hours of private coaching to improve upon their own specific skills.

Satori

atori (Sa-to-ree) is a Japanese Zen Buddhist term for enlightenment. The word literally means, "to understand." Most people refer to these moments of inspiration as their light-bulb moments. We call them *satori* moments. We encourage you to record your ideas, thoughts, and observations from the book as you read. We'd also recommend you write down the page number in the book so you can reference back to that topic. This *Satori* section can become your personal index for the *Corporate Ovations* book.

悟り

Satori

Satori

悟
り

悟り

Satori

Satori

悟
り

悟
り

Satori

_____

_____

_____

_____

_____

_____

_____

_____

_____

_____

_____

_____

_____

_____

_____

Satori

悟
り

悟り

Satori

Satori

悟り

悟り

Satori

Satori

悟
り

悟
り

Satori

Satori

悟
り

_____

_____

_____

_____

_____

_____

_____

_____

_____

_____

_____

_____

_____

_____

_____

_____

_____

悟
り

Satori

Satori

悟り

悟
り

Satori

_____

_____

_____

_____

_____

_____

_____

_____

_____

_____

_____

_____

_____

_____

_____

Endnotes

Chapter One Notes

1. Cannon, Walter Bradford. *Bodily Changes in Pain, Hunger, Fear and Rage: An Account of Recent Researches into the Function of Emotional Excitement.* Appleton-Century-Crofts, 1915.
2. Linkletter, Art. *Yes, You Can!.* Spire, 1990.
3. "Snakes Top List of Americans' Fears." http://www.gallup.com/poll/1891/snakes-top-list-americans-fears.aspx.
4. Maslow, A. H. "A Theory of Human Motivation." *Psychological Review* 50, no. 4 (1943): 370–96.
5. Walters, Lilly. *Secrets of Successful Speakers: How You Can Motivate, Captivate, and Persuade.* McGraw-Hill, 1993.
6. Carnegie, Dale. *How to Develop Self-Confidence and Influence People by Public Speaking.* Pocket Books, 1956.
7. Einstein, A. "Ist die Trägheit eines Körpers von seinem Energieinhalt abhängig?." *Annalen der Physik* 18 (1905): 639–43.
8. Weil, Andrew. *Breathing: The Master Key to Self-Healing.*
9. Watson, Burton. *The Complete Works of Chuang Tzu.* New York: Columbia University Press.
10. Mayo Foundation for Medical Education and Research. http://www.mayoclinic.com/health/HealthyLivingIndex/HealthyLivingIndex.

Chapter Two Notes

1. Wooden, John and Don Yaeger. *A Game Plan for Life: The Power of Mentoring.* 1st ed. Bloomsbury USA, 2009.
2. Waitley, Denis. *The Psychology of Winning.* Berkeley, 1986.
3. Weiss, Alan. *Million Dollar Speaking: The Professional's Guide to Building Your Platform.* 1st. ed. McGraw-Hill, 2010.
4. Festinger, L. *A Theory of Cognitive Dissonance.* Evanston, IL: Row, Peterson, 1957.

5. Cosby, Bill. *I Started Out as a Child.* Warner Bros., 1964.
6. Seinfeld, Jerry. *Seinlanguage.* Bantam, 2008.

Chapter Three Notes

1. Maxwell, John C. *Everyone Communicates, Few Connect: What the Most Effective People Do Differently.* 1st ed. Thomas Nelson, 2010.
2. Booher, Dianna. *Speak with Confidence: Powerful Presentations that Inform, Inspire and Persuade.* 1st ed. McGraw-Hill, 2002.
3. Robinson, Ken. TED Talk. http://www.ted.com/talks/ken_robinson_says_schools_kill_creativity.html. February 2006.
4. http://www.chick-fil-aleadercast.com.
5. Jeffreys, Michael. *Success Secrets of the Motivational Superstars: America's Greatest Speakers Reveal Their Secrets.* Three Rivers Press, 1996.
6. Walters, Lilly. *Secrets of Successful Speakers: How You Can Motivate, Captivate, and Persuade.* McGraw-Hill, 1993.
7. JC Anderson's Golf Lesson. http://youtu.be/osD2U-s8i6E.

Chapter Four Notes

1. McDonnel, Sharon. "Grading the C.E.O. Speech." *New York Times,* September 27, 2005.
2. Gladwell, Malcolm. *Blink: The Power of Thinking without Thinking.* Back Bay Books Publishing.
3. http://www.summit-commercial.com/principals.html.
4. http://www.howardstern.com.
5. http://www.rmhc-austin.org.
6. Aristotle. *The Rhetoric and the Poetics of Aristotle.* Translated by Rhys Roberts and Ingram Bywater. New York: Random House, Inc., 1954, 1984.
7. Berra, Yogi. *The Yogi Book.* Workman Publishing, 1998.
8. Whiting, Bartlett Jere. *Early American Proverbs and Proverbial Phrases.* Belknap Press of Harvard University Press, 1978.
9. Harvey, Paul. *The Rest of the Story.* Radio Show. ABC Radio Networks.
10. Wesson, Kenneth. "Learning & Memory: How Do We Remember and Why Do We Often Forget?." *Brain World Magazine,* March 1, 2012.
11. Giglio, Louie. *How Great Is Our God.* Six Step Records. 2012. DVD.
12. Carnegie, Dale. *How to Win Friends and Influence People.* 1936.

Chapter Five Notes

1. Covey, Stephen R. *The 7 Habits of Highly Effective People.* Revised ed. Free Press, 2004.

2. *Batman Begins.* 2005. Warner Bros. Pictures.

3. http://www.rotary.org.

4. Reagan, Ronald. Address at the Brandenburg Gate, June 12, 1987.

5. Harvey, Paul. *The Rest of the Story.* Radio Show. ABC Radio Networks.

6. http://www.xo.com.

7. Pausch, Randy. *The Last Lecture.* 1st ed. Hyperion, 2008.

8. Weissman, Jerry. *Presentations in Action: 80 Memorable Presentation Lessons from the Masters.* 1st ed. FT Press, 2011.

9. Shepherd, Jean. *A Christmas Story.* Directed by Bob Clark. 1983. Warner Bros. Pictures.

10. Gitomer, Jeffrey. *Little Red Book of Selling: 12.5 Principles of Sales Greatness.* 1st ed. Bard Press, 2004.

11. http://www.habitat.org.

12. Pausch, Randy. *Last Lecture: Achieving Your Childhood Dreams.* YouTube http://www.youtube.com/watch?v=ji5_MqicxSo.

13. Zeoli, Richard. *The 7 Principles of Public Speaking: Proven Methods from a PR Professional.* Skyhorse Publishing, 2008.

Chapter Six Notes

1. Garver, Eugene. *Aristotle's Rhetoric: An Art of Character.* 1st ed. University Of Chicago Press, 1995.
   and
   Aristotle. *Rhetoric.* Translated by W. Rhys Roberts. Indo-European Publishing, 2012.

2. Garmston, Robert J. and Bruce M. Wellman. *How to Make Presentations That Teach and Transform.* Association for Supervision & Curriculum, December 1992.

3. Bunce, D. M., E. A. Flens, and K. Y. Neiles. "How Long Can Students Pay Attention in Class? A Study of Student Attention Decline Using Clickers." *Journal of Chemical Education* 87 (2010): 1438–43.

4. Booker, Christopher. *The Seven Basic Plots: Why We Tell Stories.* 1st ed. Continuum, 2006.

5. Churchill, Winston. Address to the British House of Commons, May 14, 1940.

6. *The Wizard of Oz.* 1939. MGM—Warner Bros.

7. Cosby, Bill. *Bill Cosby: Himself.* 1983. 20th Century Fox.

8. Nagourney, Adam. "Obama Elected President as Racial Barrier Falls." *New York Times*, November 4, 2008.

9. King, Martin Luther Jr. "I Have a Dream." Address, Aug. 28, 1963.

10. Kennedy, John F. Inaugural Address, January 20, 1961.

11. Reagan, Ronald. Address at the Brandenburg Gate, June 12, 1987.

12. Matthew 5:5.

13. Heath, Chip and Dan Heath. *Made to Stick: Why Some Ideas Survive and Others Die.* 1st ed. Random House, 2007.

14. http://www.iSpeak.com.
15. http://www.ispeak.com/about/awards.
16. Goldstein, Noah J., Steve J. Martin, and Robert B. Cialdini. *Yes!: 50 Scientifically Proven Ways to Be Persuasive.* Reprint ed. Free Press, 2009.
17. Foxworthy, Jeff. *You Might Be a Redneck If...* Warner Bros. 1993.
18. Bunce, Flens, and Neiles.

Chapter Seven Notes

1. http://www.documentengine.com.
2. Heath, Chip and Dan Heath. *Made to Stick: Why Some Ideas Survive and Others Die.* 1st ed. Random House, 2007.
3. Margolis, Michael. *Believe Me: Why Your Vision, Brand, and Leadership Need a Bigger Story.* Get Storied Press, 2009.
4. Seinfeld, Jerry and David, Larry. *Seinfeld.* 1989-1998. NBC.
5. Denning, Stephen. *The Leader's Guide to Storytelling: Mastering the Art and Discipline of Business Narrative.* 1st ed. Jossey-Bass, 2005.
6. Sadoski, Mark, Ernest T. Goetz, and Joyce B. Fritz. *A Causal Model of Sentence Recall: Effects of Familiarity, Concreteness, Comprehensibility, and Interestingness.* Texas A&M University.
7. Carpenter, Humphrey *The Inklings: C. S. Lewis, J. R. R. Tolkien, Charles Williams and Their Friends.* London: George Allen & Unwin, 1978.
8. Baldwin, Christina. *Storycatcher: Making Sense of Our Lives through the Power and Practice of Story.* New World Library, 2005.
9. http://www.c-a-m.com.
10. Martin, Steve. *Born Standing Up: A Comic's Life.* 1st ed. Scribner, 2007.
11. http://www.MarkSanborn.com.
12. http://www.lionking.com.
13. Simmons, Annette. *The Story Factor.* 2nd ed. Basic Books, 2006.
14. http://www.tomclancy.com.
15. Kotter, John P. *Leading Change.* 1st ed. Harvard Business Review Press, 1996.

Chapter Eight Notes

1. Mehrabian, Albert. *Silent Messages.* 1st ed. Belmont, CA: Wadsworth, 1971.
2. Walters, Lilly. *Secrets of Successful Speakers: How You Can Motivate, Captivate, and Persuade.* McGraw-Hill, 1993. p 140.
3. Argyle, Michael. *Bodily Communication.* Revised ed. Routledge, 2010.
4. Decker, Bert. *You've Got to Be Believed to Be Heard: Reach the First Brain to Communicate in Business and in Life.* St. Martin's Griffin, 1993.
5. Wikipedia. "Greek Words for Love." Accessed 2012. http://en.wikipedia.org/wiki/Greek_words_for_love.

6. Waitley, Denis. *Wordmaster: Improve Your Word Power.* Audiobook. Your Coach in a Box, 2006.

7. http://www.languagemonitor.com/no-of-words/no-of-words. (NOTE: January 1, 2013 estimate of words in the English Language: 1,019,729.6.)

8. Carnegie, Dale. *How to Win Friends and Influence People.* Pocket Books, 1990.

9. Thorndike, Edward. "A Constant Error in Psychological Ratings." *J. Appl. Psychol.* 4, (1920): 25–29.

10. Donaldson, Les. *Conversational Magic: Key to Poise, Popularity, and Success.* Parker Publishing Company, 1981.

11. Chen, Brian X. "Get Ready for 1 Billion Smartphones by 2016, Forrester Says." *New York Times*, February 13, 2012.

12. http://www.toastmasters.org.

13. Chambers, Harry E. *Effective Communication Skills for Scientific and Technical Professionals.* Basic Books, 2000.

14. "She's Worried About Awkward Silence." *Boston Globe*, February 16, 1993.

15. Humes, James C. *Speak Like Churchill, Stand Like Lincoln: 21 Powerful Secrets of History's Greatest Speakers.* 1st edition. Three Rivers Press, 2002.

16. Valentine, Craig. "Five Ways to Master the Pause." Blog Post. December 14th, 2011. http://www.craigvalentine.com/5-ways-to-master-the-pause.

17. *Titanic.* Directed by James Cameron. 1997. 20th Century Fox and Paramount Pictures.

18. *Braveheart.* Directed by Mel Gibson. 1995. Paramount Pictures.

Chapter Nine Notes

1. Philpott, Jeffrey S. "The Relative Contribution to Meaning of Verbal and Nonverbal Channels of Communication." Unpublished Master's Project, University of Nebraska-Lincoln, 1983.

2. *The Brady Bunch.* 1969–1974. Paramount Television.

3. Blanchard, Kenneth. *Whale Done!: The Power of Positive Relationships.* 1st ed. Free Press, 2002.

4. Gladwell, Malcolm. *Blink: The Power of Thinking without Thinking.* 1st ed. Little, Brown and Company, 2005.

5. *The Price Is Right.* 1972-Present. CBS Television.

6. Hamilton, Cheryl. *Communicating for Results, A Guide for Business and the Professions.* 8th ed. Wadsworth Publishing Company, 2007.

7. Caird, John. *Theatre Craft: A Director's Practical Companion from A-Z.* 1st ed. Faber & Faber, 2010.

8. Journey. *Frontiers.* Columbia Records, 1983.

9. Weissman, Jerry. *The Power Presenter: Technique, Style, and Strategy from America's Top Speaking Coach.* 1st ed. Wiley, 2009.

10. ScienceDaily. "Hand Gestures Linked to Better Speaking." Posted May 11, 2005. http://www.sciencedaily.com/releases/2005/05/050511105253.htm.

11. https://paulekman.com/face.
    and
    Lie to Me. 2009-2011. Imagine Entertainment and 20th Century FOX Television.
12. Ekman, P., and W. V. Friesen. "Constants Across Cultures in the Face and Emotion." *Journal of Personality and Social Psychology* 17 (1971): 124–29.
13. Carnegie, Dale. *How to Win Friends and Influence People.* Reissue ed. Simon & Schuster, 2009.
14. Duchenne de Boulogne, G. B., and Andrew R. Cuthbertson. *The Mechanism of Human Facial Expression.* Cambridge, UK; New York: Cambridge University Press, 1990. p. 227.
15. Uba, L. *Asian Americans: Personality Patterns, Identity, and Mental Health.* New York: Guilford Press, 1994.
16. Wierzbicka, Anna. "Russian Emotional Expression. *Ethos* 26 (1998): 456–83. Accessed April 4, 2008. JSTOR database.
17. Ekman, Paul. *Emotions Revealed: Recognizing Faces and Feelings to Improve Communication and Emotional Life.* 2nd ed. Holt Paperbacks, 2007.
18. Decker, Bert. *You've Got to Be Believed to Be Heard: Reach the First Brain to Communicate in Business and in Life.* St. Martin's Griffin, 1993.
19. Reynolds, Garr. *The Naked Presenter: Delivering Powerful Presentations With or Without Slides.* 1st ed. New Riders, 2010.

Chapter Ten Notes

1. Garber, Angela R. "Death by PowerPoint." Posted April 2001. http://www.smallbusinesscomputing.com/biztools/article.php/684871/ Death-By-Powerpoint.htm.
2. Reynolds, Garr. *Presentation Zen: Simple Ideas on Presentation Design and Delivery.* New Riders Press, 2008.
3. Construction Safety and Health Outreach Program. OSHA Office of Training and Education. US Department of Labor. May 1996. www.osha.gov
4. Silver, Harvey F., Richard W. Strong, and Matthew J. Perini. *So Each May Learn: Integrating Learning Styles and Multiple Intelligences.* Association for Supervision & Curriculum Development, 2000.
5. Weiss, Alan. *Money Talks: How to Make a Million as a Speaker.* 1st ed. McGraw-Hill, 1997.
6. Wikipedia. "Ludwig Mies van der Rohe." Accessed 2012. http://en.wikipedia.org/ wiki/Ludwig_Mies_van_der_Rohe.
7. Gallagher. *The Best of Gallagher, Volume 3.* ANCHOR BAY, 2007. DVD.
8. http://www.youtube.com/corporateovations.
9. Handford, Martin. *Where's Waldo?.* 2nd ed. Candlewick Publishers, 1997.
10. MindWorks Resources. http://www.mindworksresources.com/p-324-3-primary-learning-modalities-every-person-uses.aspx.
11. Levie, W. H., and R. Lentz. "The Effects of Text Illustrations: A Review of Research." *Educational Communication and Technology Journal* 30 (1982): 195–232.

12. Duarte, Nancy. *slide:ology: The Art and Science of Creating Great Presentations.* O'Reilly Media, 2008.

13. *Mac Life Magazine*, July 2007. p 84.

14. http://www.steveuzzell.com/speaker.html.

15. http://www.pecha-kucha.org/what. 2003.

16. Guffey, Mary Ellen. *Business Communication: Process and Product.* 6th ed. South-Western College Publication, 2007.

17. http://prezi.com.

Chapter Eleven Notes

1. Freese, Thomas. *Secrets of Question Based Selling: How the Most Powerful Tool in Business Can Double Your Sales Results.* Sourcebooks, Inc., 2000.

2. Thurber, James. "The Scotty Who Knew Too Much." In *Fables for Our Time and Famous Poems Illustrated*, 28. Harper Perennial, 1983.

3. Asher, Joey. *15 Minutes Including Q&A: A Plan to Save the World From Lousy Presentations.* 1st ed. Persuasive Speaker Press, 2010.

4. Kessler, Daniella. *Observations.* AuthorHouse, 2009.

5. Handey, Jack. *Deep Thoughts.* Berkley Trade, 1992.

6. Richardson, Linda. *Stop Telling, Start Selling: How to Use Customer-Focused Dialogue to Close Sales.* McGraw-Hill, 1998.

7. Esar, Evan. *20,000 Quips & Quotes, A Treasury of Witty Remarks, Comic Proverbs, Wisecracks, and Epigrams.* Barnes & Noble Books, 1995.

Chapter Twelve Notes

1. National Park Service. "History of the Statue of Liberty." www.statueofliberty.org/Statue_History.html.

2. Kelly, Thomas. *The Back Stage Guide to Stage Management: Traditional and New Methods for Running a Show from First Rehearsal to Last Performance.* 1999.

3. Gladwell, Malcolm. Outliers: The Story of Success, Malcolm Gladwell, 2011, Back Bay Books.

4. Brynie, Faith. "The Madness of Multitasking: 'Think you're getting more done when you multitask? Think again.'" *Psychology Today.* Published in *Brain Sense.* August 24, 2009.

5. Apple, Inc. "There's an App for Everything." 2009. (NOTE: This is a trademark advertising slogan used by Apple, Inc. to advertise the iPhone and iPad.)

6. Allen, Steve. *How to Make a Speech.* McGraw-Hill, 1986.

7. Wright, Steven. *I Have a Pony.* WEA International. 1987.

8. Wikipedia. "Tiger Woods." http://en.wikipedia.org/wiki/Tiger_Woods.

9. Schmoker, Mike. *Focus: Elevating the Essentials to Radically Improve Student Learning.* Association for Supervision & Curriculum Development, 2011.

Implement to Improve Notes

1. Gladwell, Malcolm. *Outliers: The Story of Success.* Little, Brown and Company, 2008.
2. Schwartz-Hebron, Reut. *The Art and Science of Changing People Who Don't Want to Change.* 1st ed. Real House Press, 2012.
3. Maltz, Maxwell. *Psycho-Cybernetics, A New Way to Get More Living Out of Life.* Pocket Books, 1989.
4. http://www.childrenatheartministries.org/.
5. Harford, Tim. *Adapt: Why Success Always Starts with Failure.* Picador, 2012.

Index